C000102376

FRANCISCO
in your pocket

MICHELIN
Travel Publications

PHOTOGRAPH CREDITS
Photos supplied by The Travel Library:
title page; Berkeley Convention & Visitors Center 92;
Stuart Black 35, 54, 63, 101; Maxine Cass 9, 10, 12, 16,
32, 43, 44, 96; Heather Coulson 72; Ecoscene 83, 85;
Greg Evans 90; M J Macleod 115; Rob Moore front
cover, back cover, 5, 6, 14, 15, 17, 18, 19, 21, 24, 25, 27,
28, 29, 30(t,b), 31, 33(t,b), 37, 38, 41, 45, 46, 49, 51, 53,
55, 56, 58, 60, 64, 66, 67, 69, 70, 71, 73, 74, 76, 79, 86, 87,
89, 95, 99, 100, 103, 104, 107, 109, 111, 119, 125; Suellen
Raven 81.

*Front cover: Golden Gate Bridge; back cover: Yerba Buena
Gardens; title page: the Transamerica Pyramid and Columbus
Tower.*

MANUFACTURE FRANÇAISE DES PNEUMATIQUES MICHELIN

Place des Carmes-Déchaux – 63000 Clermont-Ferrand (France)

© Michelin et Cie. Propriétaires-Éditeurs 1999

Dépôt légal Mars 99 – ISBN 2-06-653001-8 – ISSN 1272-1689

No part of this publication may be reproduced in any form
without the prior permission of the publisher.

Printed in Spain 1-00/2

MICHELIN TYRE PLC
Travel Publications
The Edward Hyde Building
38 Clarendon Road
WATFORD Herts WD1 1SX - UK
☎ (01923) 415000

MICHELIN TRAVEL PUBLICATIONS
Editorial Department
One Parkway South
GREENVILLE, SC 29615
☎ 1-800 423-0485

CONTENTS

INTRODUCTION

San Francisco is the very essence of the modern American West. Located at the heart of the California coast, it's a dynamic city which persists at the cutting edge of change while refusing to dismiss its colorful past.

First settled by Spanish Catholic missionaries from Mexico in the 18C, this thumb of land, surrounded on three sides by water, boomed with the discovery of California gold in the mid 19C. Fortunes made by urban entrepreneurs stayed in the city to give it a grand landscape of hotels and theaters, broad parks and handsome mansions, and a cable car system that dared to conquer the imposing hills. San Francisco became the financial center of the Far West and was considered one of the world's great cities when, in 1906, it was destroyed by a tremendous earthquake and fire.

Undeterred, resilient citizens rebuilt San Francisco and restaked their claim to greatness. After the Second World War, the city became a magnet for the counterculture. Young Americans who could venture no further west by land became the North Beach beatniks of the 1950s, the Haight-Ashbury hippies of the late '60s and early '70s, and the gay community which burgeoned in the Castro District in the later '70s. The lasting impact of these various groups can best be felt in the cultural life of San Francisco: its visual and performing arts, its music and literature.

Today, no visitor would dream of missing the magnificent Golden Gate Bridge, bustling Fisherman's Wharf nor colorful Chinatown. But there's much more to San Francisco. Ride the cable car up steep Russian Hill and descend on foot down twisting Lombard Street, 'the crookedest street in the world'. Spend a day in the wonderful museums of Golden Gate Park.

Relax with a cup of espresso on Columbus Avenue and watch the ghosts of writers Jack Kerouac and Allen Ginsberg glide past.

Then get out of town. Drive north across the Golden Gate Bridge to visit the rugged coastline of Marin County and, beyond, the wine country of the Napa and Sonoma valleys. Head east, across San Francisco Bay, to the impressive campus of the University of California, or south along the coast to wondrous Pacific marine wildlife refuges.

This is one of those rare cities that remains with you long after your journey has come to an end. Through lingering memories, you will understand why millions have left their hearts in San Francisco.

Traffic zigzags down through colorful displays on Lombard Street, 'The crookedest street in the world'.

GEOGRAPHY

'The coldest winter I ever spent,' novelist Mark Twain once said, 'was a summer in San Francisco.' Twain exaggerated, as was his fashion, but it's no stretch to say this city can experience four seasons in a single day. That's a function of its unique geography.

San Francisco occupies the 7 mile- (11km-) wide tip of a long peninsula. To the west is the **Pacific Ocean**, to the east the great harbor known as **San Francisco Bay**. The two are

linked north of the city by the 1.2 mile-
(1.9km-) wide Golden Gate passage. The
Coastal Range, a low, rugged belt of mountains
stretching from Santa Barbara County to
Oregon, run through San Francisco and the
Bay Area, and the city is spread across these
hills and valleys. San Francisco's famed steep
streets climb rapidly to the summit, then
plunge alarmingly on the other side. Further
east, the **Sierra Nevada** range blocks cold
continental air masses from reaching the coast,
where ocean breezes moderate temperature
extremes.

In fact, this city has the lowest average
summer temperature (even in August, the daily
average is only 59°F/15°C) of any American
city outside of Alaska, yet no significant snow
has fallen in more than a century. As a rule,
summers are cool and dry, winters wet and
mild. Yet the hilly promontory – no cape of
windswept sand – has a tendency to foster
microclimates. It's not impossible for the
Embarcadero, on the inland bay, to be baking
in 78°F (26°C) heat while Land's End,
overlooking the ocean, is suffering through a
43°F (6°C). The **fog** is especially prevalent
in summer. It does not creep in 'on little cat
feet'. Quite to the contrary, San Francisco's
thick banks of fog build along the coast before
pouring through the Golden Gate and into the
Bay in the afternoons, leaving higher hilltops
as islands in a sea of gray-white.

Far underground, the Pacific and North
American plates of the earth's crust slide
against each other in a series of tectonic faults
that give rise to frequent **earthquakes.** The
largest of the faults, the San Andreas, which
passes under the seabed just off San Francisco's
Pacific shore, has been responsible for the
worst tremors, including those of 1906 and
1989.

San Francisco and
the Golden Gate
Bridge, seen from
Marin Headlands.

HISTORY

Ohlone and Miwok Indians were the Bay area's original residents. Between 7 000 and 10 000 hunters and gatherers lived in relative harmony until the Spanish arrived in the 18C.

The first tentative **European exploration** of this coast had begun with the Spanish Juan Rodríguez Cabrillo in 1542. Englishman Francis Drake landed on the northern California shore in 1579 and claimed the country for Queen Elizabeth I. But no settlements were attempted until 1769 when Franciscan **Father Junípero Serra** built the first of 21 missions along El Camino Real, 'The King's Highway' from San Diego to Sonoma. The Spanish established a provincial capital at Monterey; it was this bay for which Sgt José Ortega was searching when his scouting party inadvertently stumbled upon San Francisco Bay, naming it after St Francis.

A military garrison, the Presidio, was founded in 1776 on a hill overlooking the bay's entrance. A few miles south, Mission San Francisco de Asis was erected. Located on the Laguna de los Dolores, '**Mission Dolores,**' as it became known, was the focus for colonizing and pacifying natives by converting them to Roman Catholicism and teaching them agriculture and related trades. When Mexico declared its independence from Spain in 1821, missions were removed from church control and native lands quickly absorbed by powerful private landholders.

The founding father of the modern city of San Francisco was **William Richardson**, an English sailor who jumped ship here in 1822. Richardson married the daughter of a Presidio commander, became a Mexican citizen and Roman Catholic convert, and in 1835 built a shanty home (soon replaced by a two-story adobe) and trading post on a hillside above Yerba Buena Cove, on the bayshore. Other adobes followed, and within a decade the village of **Yerba Buena** ('good herb' in Spanish, a phrase that did not escape later marijuana-smoking hippies) had grown into a bustling town of 800 Americans, Spanish, Dutch, Hawaiians and West Indians.

American Riches

Two events propelled Yerba Buena (renamed San Francisco in 1847) into the second half of the 19C. The first was the **Mexican War**. Americans in Sonoma declared California's independence in 1846; less than a month later the US flag was raised above the Bay. California and other Mexican real estate was formally ceded to the US by the **Treaty of Guadalupe Hidalgo** on 2 February 1848.

Just nine days earlier, on 24 January, a construction foreman, building a sawmill in the Sierra Nevada foothills, had discovered **gold** in the American River. Within a year, gold-seekers from all over the world descended like locusts upon San Francisco; its population swelled a hundredfold to 90 000. By 1852, fully one-third of the **Forty-Niners**, as they were called, had given up the goldfields and become permanent residents of the city. San Francisco became the fourth largest harbor city in the United States.

In 1859, San Francisco was visited by a second wave of good fortune when a fabulously rich vein of silver, the **Comstock Lode**, was discovered east of Lake Tahoe. Easterners found it more attractive to take a ship to San Francisco and travel 250 miles (400km)

The Forty-Niners, who flooded into the country in the Gold Rush of 1849, are depicted on the base of this street lamp.

San Francisco is renowned for its late-19C cable car system, still going strong today.

to the silver workings of Virginia City, Nevada, than to make an overland wagon journey of several months. The city was not slow to take advantage of the sudden influx of prospectors, all of whom had to be fed, housed and supplied.

The ensuing wave of growth included the city's signature **cable car system**. A rectangular grid had been planned as early as 1847 without regard to San Francisco's peculiar topography: streets abruptly ascended and crested steep hills, then plummeted down the other sides. Scottish engineer Andrew Hallidie's cable car, unveiled in 1873, enabled residential conquest of the heights. By 1890, eight different lines with 600 cars and more than 100 miles (160km) of track crisscrossed the city. (Today, 40 restored cable cars still operate on three distinct lines.)

On Track and Off
The cable car followed on the heels of America's first **transcontinental railroad**. Employing more than 15 000 Chinese workers, construction of the Central Pacific Railroad began from Sacramento in 1863 and met the westbound Union Pacific in 1869, near the

Great Salt Lake. The rail system made vast fortunes for '**The Big Four**' Sacramento businessmen – Leland Stanford, Mark Hopkins, Collis P Huntingdon and Charles Crocker – who financed the project and turned their partnership into the most powerful political machine in the West.

Chinese gold seekers and rail workers established the foundation for San Francisco's **Chinatown**. By 1880, some 50 000 had settled in the densely populated blocks flanking Grant Avenue. Although the immigrants were denied citizenship, land ownership and most civil liberties, they were highly successful in business. Beneath its colorful skin, however, Chinatown became a haven for vice and organized crime – opium and other drugs, gambling and prostitution – ruled by a handful of warring 'tongs', or secret societies.

A few blocks north, at the foot of Telegraph Hill, the **Barbary Coast** strip was notorious among sailors and con artists the world over. Naive tourists who ventured into rowdy saloons could find themselves shanghaied upon boats to China or sold into white slavery.

But even in desperate times, San Francisco wore a face that fostered its reputation as the **Paris of the West**. Visits by European opera companies and world-famous stage performers nurtured the high spark of the well-heeled. Writers like Mark Twain and Rudyard Kipling, Robert Louis Stevenson and Jack London honed their literary talents in the Bay Area.

A Phoenix From the Ashes

It seemed as if nothing less than an act of God could quell San Francisco's inexorable spirit, its extravagance and sinfulness. Some argue that's exactly what happened shortly after 5am, 18 April 1906, when the San Andreas Fault slipped 21ft (6.4m) in a matter of seconds.

The massive **earthquake**, later estimated at 8.3 on the Richter Scale, destroyed tenement apartments, a hospital and City Hall. Many other structures survived relatively unscathed, but by noon, broken gas mains had ignited 52 fires around the city. With the urban water supply severed, firefighters could do little but watch San Francisco burn … for three days. In all, 674 people were dead or missing, 250 000 (nearly two-thirds of the population) homeless, and 514 blocks of homes and offices, factories and warehouses, churches and schools destroyed.

Not devastated was the city's spirit. Relief funds poured in from around the world and **reconstruction** proceeded with phenomenal speed. In 1915, San Francisco celebrated its miraculous recovery by hosting the **Panama-Pacific International Exposition**.

Indeed, the earthquake had been a sort of spiritual cleansing. The Barbary Coast had vanished like a modern Gomorrah, corruption had been weeded out, and San Francisco, spearheaded by five-term (1911-31) **Mayor 'Sunny Jim' Rolph**, entered a new era of progressive growth. Not even labor strife during the Great Depression of the 1930s could retard the city. Coit Tower was built atop Telegraph Hill and Alcatraz Island was made a maximum-security federal penitentiary. With the completion of the San Francisco-Oakland Bay Bridge and the Golden Gate Bridge, the city's long dependence on ferries was eliminated.

San Francisco's brave volunteer firemen are remembered in North Beach.

12

Frenzy and Flamboyance

As America's major Pacific port, San Francisco was thrown headlong into the **Second World War** when the Japanese bombed Pearl Harbor. Nearly 2 million soldiers and 23 million tons of war supplies passed through the city between the end of 1941 and the late summer of 1945. The industrial civilian workforce more than doubled in size. By the time the war ended – and the charter of the new United Nations was drafted and signed in San Francisco – the city's population had exploded to more than three-quarters of a million people.

After the frenzy of wartime activity, San Francisco was eclipsed by Los Angeles as California's manufacturing hub, and the population plateaued and even fell slightly. But the city retained its flamboyant and eccentric character. Always tolerant of unconventional thought, San Francisco gave birth to a series of '**counterculture**' **movements** (see p.14).

A wave of new construction transformed the city skyline in the early 1970s. But the **Loma Prieta earthquake** of 1989, which buckled freeways in Oakland and destroyed homes in the Marina District, reminded San Franciscans that existence on their hilly peninsula is precarious indeed. That's all the more reason to live life to its fullest … something at which San Franciscans are exceptionally good.

PEOPLE AND CULTURE

San Francisco's three quarters of a million residents are a truly diverse group. Even today, fully one-third of them are foreign-born, and half of the remainder are not native Californians. Census figures break the city's population down as 47% non-Hispanic white, 28% Asian, 14% Latino and 11% African-American.

The Counterculture

A series of offbeat 'counter-cultural' movements have had their cradles in San Francisco, beginning in the 1950s with the bohemian Beat Generation. Dubbed '**beatniks**' by revered newspaper columnist Herb Caen, their numbers – including disaffected poets Allen Ginsberg and Lawrence Ferlinghetti, and novelists Jack Kerouac and William Burroughs – congregated in the Italian coffee houses of North Beach, reading from their works and pondering the meaning of life. (City Lights Bookstore, which Ferlinghetti opened on Columbus Avenue in 1953 and continues to own, still features

City Lights Bookstore.

space for public readings and has an extensive selection of Beat Generation writings.)

In the mid 1960s, the Haight-Ashbury district, a Victorian neighborhood on the east side of Golden Gate Park, became home to the '**hippies**'. Encouraged by drug-culture prophets like Dr Timothy Leary, whose 'Tune in, turn on, drop out' philosophy became a mantra for the era, and by holdover beatniks like Ginsberg, who by now was experimenting with Asian mysticism and mass gatherings he called 'be-ins,' the pacifistic 'flower children' challenged traditional values with their long hair, patchy clothes, and belief in free love and casual drug use. Along the way they spawned a whole new genre of music as represented by such rock performers as Janis Joplin, Jefferson Airplane and the Grateful Dead.

Coinciding with the hippie movement was the rise of the **New Left**, centered on the University of California in Berkeley. Many leftists wore long hair, beards and other marks of hippiedom, but their values were far more confrontational. Taking on such issues as racism,

THE COUNTERCULTURE

poverty and especially the war in Vietnam, Berkeley's protesters spawned a movement that spread across the US and Europe. Local offshoots included the militant Black Panthers and quirky Symbionese Liberation Army, which made headlines when it kidnapped newspaper heiress Patty Hearst. The New Left faded after the US withdrawal from Vietnam in 1975, but it made a mark on American politics that remains to this day.

San Francisco's reputation for political and social tolerance also inspired thousands of homosexual men and women to move to the city. By the mid 1970s, an overtly **gay community** had developed in a former blue-collar neighborhood on Castro Street. In 1977, Harvey Milk was elected by his peers to the city's Board of Supervisors, becoming the first openly gay elected official in American history. Milk and Mayor George Moscone were shot and killed the following year by a disgruntled former supervisor, but by then the gay community wielded sufficient political power to spur the passage of a formal Gay Bill of Civil Rights, forbidding discrimination in housing and employment on the basis of sexual orientation. When the the AIDS epidemic created a panic in the Castro in the 1980s, residents responded by creating a network of public-education and support groups.

Gay Pride March.

BACKGROUND

Past and future faces of Chinatown are portrayed in this Darryl Mar mural.

Among the whites, nearly half are of British-Irish ancestry, with large additional groups of German, Italian and French heritage. Italian influence is evident in the restaurants and coffee shops of North Beach. Nearly two-thirds of Asians are of Chinese ancestry; their principal enclave is Chinatown and surrounding neighborhoods like Nob Hill, Russian Hill and North Beach. A majority of Latinos (mainly Mexicans and Salvadorans) live in the Mission District and other South of Market communities.

About 40% of San Francisco residents are single; nearly 60% have at least some college education. They have a strong interest in the arts, which thrive at all levels of society. Fine dining is a passion for citizens, who are forever seeking new cuisines and creative restaurants. But they enjoy working off their calories as well, and weekends find them jogging, hiking, biking and sailing, taking advantage of the waters and extensive parklands surrounding their city.

The Bay Area is renowned as a **center for the arts,** including performing and fine arts and architecture. Throughout its history, San Francisco has nurtured the classical traditions of opera, symphony and ballet, while making room for Chinese opera, Latin jazz and ethnic dance.

It emerged as a jazz hub in the 1950s, a rock-and-roll mecca in the 1960s. Theater has thrived since gold-rush days, when Shakespeare was as popular as circus acts and minstrel shows. Today the American Conservatory Theater is ranked among the best regional theaters and drama schools in the US.

The roots of San Francisco's multilayered **art history** lie in native Indian basketry and Mexican religious art. European values and aesthetics were introduced during and after the 1849 Gold Rush. Arts and Crafts and Tonalist movements were influential in the early 20C, while abstract expressionism and Bay Area figurative emerged after the Second World War. Regional artists' works are well represented at numerous museums, including the new San Francisco Museum of Modern Art and the Oakland Museum of California in the East Bay.

The city's most enduring **architectural** trademarks are its Victorian homes, most of them built 1870-1906. Crowded together on narrow hillside lots west of Van Ness Avenue, these middle-class homes are of three main styles: Italianate, marked by neo-classical ornament and false gables; Stick or Eastlake, with flat wall surfaces and geometrically framed bay windows; and Queen Anne, a free-form and asymmetrical style incorporating corner towers or turrets. They are dubbed 'painted ladies' because of the flamboyant color schemes given them by late-20C owners.

Haight-Ashbury is the focus of fine Victorian houses.

17

EXPLORING SAN FRANCISCO

HOW TO SEE THE CITY

One of the best things about a visit to San Francisco is that you probably won't need a car to get around.

As long as you don't mind hills, San Francisco is a wonderful city for walkers. A captive of peninsula geography, it is finite in scope and thus more manageably conceived and visited than many other cities. Most attractions lie no more than two miles from one another in the north-east quadrant of the city. And when the streets get too steep to climb on foot, it's easy to hop aboard a cable car or take a bus.

The city's best choice of hotels is in the vicinity of Union Square. We recommend that

At 904ft (275m), Twin Peaks is almost the highest land in San Francisco, with panoramas over the city to the Bay Bridge beyond.

you establish a base here. Chinatown, Nob Hill, the Financial District and Market Street are no more than a few blocks distant; North Beach, Russian Hill and Fisherman's Wharf are only slightly further, and the latter two areas are readily accessed by cable car.

To travel a bit further from the core – to Golden Gate Park, for instance, or to Mission Dolores – we suggest you rely on the low-cost buses or streetcars of the San Francisco Municipal Railway (Muni). The Bay Area Rapid Transit (BART) rail line will whisk you quickly to the East Bay communities of Berkeley and Oakland. The only time you're likely to want a rental car is when you head north across the Golden Gate to Marin County or the Wine Country.

Hop onto a cable car when the gradients get too much; this one at Chestnut Street offers views across the Bay to Alcatraz.

EXPLORING SAN FRANCISCO

MUST SEE

Chinatown★★★

Stroll down **Grant Avenue★★**, the heart of one of the largest Chinese settlements outside Asia, to immerse yourself in a world of exotic shops and markets, restaurants, temples, maybe even an indigenous festival.

Lombard Street★★★

'The crookedest street in the world', on the slope of Russian Hill between Hyde and Leavenworth streets, is a one-lane avenue with eight hairpin turns profusely landscaped with bright flowers and shrubs.

Fisherman's Wharf★★★

The waterfront for several blocks east from Hyde Street is a tourist spectacle. A carnivalesque mood prevails, with street performers and souvenir shops, novelty museums and a multitude of indoor and open-air seafood eateries.

Alcatraz★★★

The infamous prison, converted to a national park and museum in 1972, occupies a 12-acre (5ha) 'rock' surrounded by San Francisco Bay. Ferries depart from Pier 41 at Fisherman's Wharf.

Coit Tower★★★

One of San Francisco's best-known landmarks, this fluted concrete shaft, built on Telegraph Hill in 1934, honors the city's firefighters. The **views★★** from its summit are magnificent.

Golden Gate Bridge★★★

This graceful suspension bridge is San Francisco's most beloved symbol. Painted a vibrant orange, it spans the bay entrance via twin towers and an intricate tracery of cables that support a 1.6 mile (2.6km) roadway.

Golden Gate Park★★★

Grant Avenue, Chinatown, is a vibrant, exotic experience.

Stretching inland from Ocean Beach, this broad rectangle – the largest cultivated urban park in the US – is home to a complex of art and science museums including the **Asian Art Museum★★★**.

Map of San Francisco

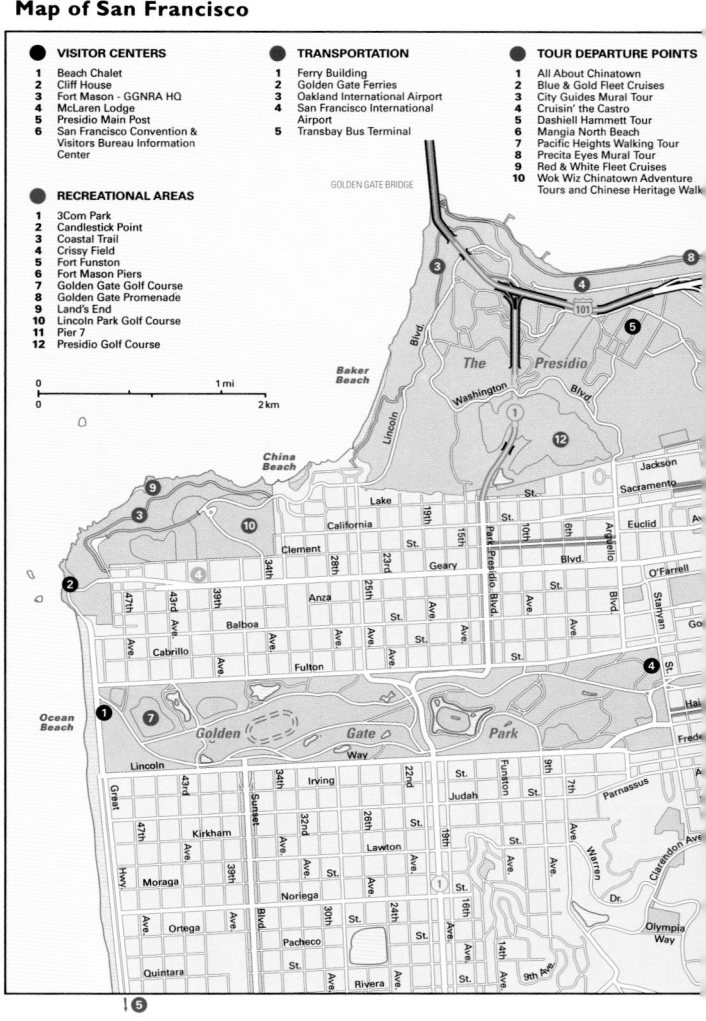

● VISITOR CENTERS
1 Beach Chalet
2 Cliff House
3 Fort Mason - GGNRA HQ
4 McLaren Lodge
5 Presidio Main Post
6 San Francisco Convention &
  Visitors Bureau Information
  Center

● RECREATIONAL AREAS
1 3Com Park
2 Candlestick Point
3 Coastal Trail
4 Crissy Field
5 Fort Funston
6 Fort Mason Piers
7 Golden Gate Golf Course
8 Golden Gate Promenade
9 Land's End
10 Lincoln Park Golf Course
11 Pier 7
12 Presidio Golf Course

● TRANSPORTATION
1 Ferry Building
2 Golden Gate Ferries
3 Oakland International Airport
4 San Francisco International
  Airport
5 Transbay Bus Terminal

● TOUR DEPARTURE POINTS
1 All About Chinatown
2 Blue & Gold Fleet Cruises
3 City Guides Mural Tour
4 Cruisin' the Castro
5 Dashiell Hammett Tour
6 Mangia North Beach
7 Pacific Heights Walking Tour
8 Precita Eyes Mural Tour
9 Red & White Fleet Cruises
10 Wok Wiz Chinatown Adventure
   Tours and Chinese Heritage Walk

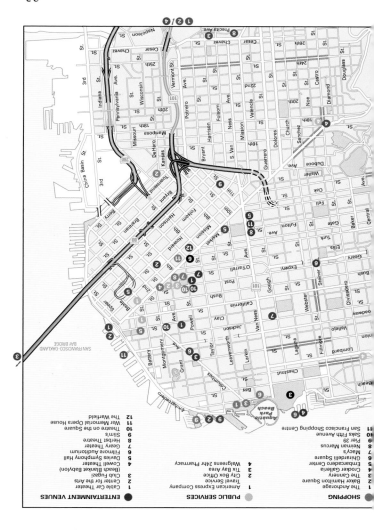

SAN FRANCISCO-OAKLAND BAY BRIDGE

MAP

SHOPPING

1	The Anchorage
2	Baker Hamilton Square
3	The Cannery
4	Crocker Galleria
5	Embarcadero Center
6	Ghirardelli Square
7	Macy's
8	Neiman Marcus
9	Pier 39
10	Saks Fifth Avenue
11	San Francisco Shopping Centre

PUBLIC SERVICES

1	American Express Company
2	Travel Service
3	City Box Office
3	Tix Bay Area
4	Walgreens 24hr Pharmacy

ENTERTAINMENT VENUES

1	Cable Car Theater
2	Center for the Arts
3	Club Fugazi (Beach Blanket Babylon)
4	Cowell Theater
5	Davies Symphony Hall
6	Fillmore Auditorium
7	Geary Theater
8	Herbst Theatre
9	Slim's
10	Theatre on the Square
11	War Memorial Opera House
12	The Warfield

DOWNTOWN AND WATERFRONT

Union Square*

The bustling Union Square area is San Francisco's most vibrant and prestigious urban shopping district. Major department stores like Macy's, Saks Fifth Avenue and Neiman Marcus mix with upmarket boutiques and art galleries, and chic cafés set up umbrella-shaded tables in secluded pedestrian lanes.

Facing the west side of the central plaza is the **Westin St Francis Hotel★★**, an elegant Renaissance-style hotel completed in 1904 and rebuilt two years later after the quake. The grand lobby of the city's largest hotel (1 900-rooms) offers a glimpse of its luxury with marble-sheathed Corinthian columns, coffered ceiling and ornate balconies.

The St Francis is at the south-east corner of the four-square-block **Theater District**, whose

Westin St Francis Hotel, Union Square – haunt of royalty, the rich and famous.

stages range from spare upstairs rooms to enormous, multibalconied palaces. Among the latter, both on Geary St, are the **Geary Theater★**, built in 1909, and the adjacent **Curran Theatre★**, opened in 1922; both are listed as National Historic Landmarks.

Extending from the east side of Union Square is the narrow (and ironically named) **Maiden Lane**, once the infamous home of a row of brothels. After the 1906 quake it was reborn as a quaint pedestrian walkway lined with maple trees and fine shops. **Folk Art International★** (140 Maiden Lane) is the only building in the city designed by renowned architect Frank Lloyd Wright (in 1948).

Chinatown★★★

Turn left where Maiden Lane meets Grant Ave and stroll uphill for just over two blocks to **Chinatown Gate**, a ceremonial portal which marks the entrance to North America's oldest

Chinatown Gate, unveiled in 1970, was designed by Chinese-American architect Clayton Lee.

and largest Chinatown. A densely packed population of 30 000 lives in the 24-square-block core of this neighborhood, which spreads along the lower eastern slope of Nob Hill overlooking the Financial District.

Although the Chinese community is now spread throughout the Bay Area, old Chinatown remains a teeming fusion of Cantonese market town and American main street. The lively shops, groceries and restaurants are de facto cultural centers for the Asians, who satisfy their medical requirements at herbalists' shops and acupuncturists' offices, and their spiritual needs at temples espousing a characteristic amalgam of Taoism, Buddhism and Confucianism.

Grant Avenue★★ comprises Chinatown's main thoroughfare for visitors. Painted balconies, curved tile roof-lines, staggered towers and dazzling color schemes give the street an exotic cachet. Shops seduce with curios in all price ranges, while restaurants serve up a delectable variety of regional cuisines, ranging from Mandarin and Hunanese to bite-size *dim sum.*

Chinatown's busiest outdoor common is **Portsmouth Square**★, central plaza of the original settlement of Yerba Buena. It was the site (in 1848) of the raising of the US flag over California, but its importance waned after the city's commercial center shifted. Today, you'll find elderly Chinese men huddled around the square playing chess and mah-jongg.

Around a corner to the south-east is the **Pacific Heritage Museum**, which features changing exhibits of Asian and Asian-American art.

A warren of side streets between Grant Ave and hectic Stockton St promote the dark intrigue of old Chinatown. In the late 19C, these alleyways saw the bloodshed of tong wars.

The Norras Temple is just one of several incense-filled temples occupying upper floor rooms on Waverly Place.

Today you may hear the hum of clothing factories and the bustle of establishments like the tiny **Golden Gate Fortune Cookie Company★** in Ross Alley, where workers bake cookies and stuff them with 'fortunes'.

The most colorful alley is **Waverly Place★**, called 'the Street of Painted Balconies' for the brightly hued decks of its Edwardian brick buildings. A host of now-benign tongs are located here, often alive with percussive sounds that emanate from behind closed doors. You'll be welcomed to third- and fourth-floor temples like the **Tin How Temple** (established in 1852 and devoted to the protector of seafarers), the **Norras Temple★** (dominated by a large gilded Buddha statue), and the **Kong Chow Temple★** (whose superb mid-19C wood carvings were moved to its present location two decades ago). Just don't forget to offer a donation to the gods.

Nob Hill★★

From Grant Ave, take the cable car (California Street Line) west for two steep blocks to the summit of 376ft- (115m-) high Nob Hill. One of the city's early posh neighborhoods, the hill

was named after the wealthy 'nabobs' who built their mansions atop this eyrie in the 1870s. These estates were razed in the 1906 fire.

The best surviving example of turn-of-the-century luxury is the elaborate main lobby of the **Fairmont Hotel★★**, which was nearing completion when the 1906 quake struck; it was promptly restored and completed in its original Italian Renaissance style. In 1945, the United Nations Charter was drafted in the hotel. The Fairmont's Crown Room restaurant offers great panoramic views of the city, as does the swank Top of the Mark bar in the adjacent **Mark Hopkins Inter-Continental Hotel**. Facing upon nearby tended Huntington Park,

From the height of Nob Hill, looking down California Street, you can catch a glimpse of the San Francisco-Oakland Bay Bridge beyond.

Take a long, lingering look at San Francisco's astonishing cityscape over a delicious American cocktail or perhaps a meal...

Start the day the t'ai chi way, in front of Grace Cathedral, Nob Hill.

a couple of blocks west, are the French Gothic spires of **Grace Cathedral**★, third-largest Episcopal (Anglican) cathedral in the US. Its eastern portal features the Gates of Paradise, 16ft- (5m-) high Florentine doors divided into ten cast-bronze panels that illustrate Old Testament scenes.

Two blocks north of the Fairmont, on Mason St, is the **Cable Car Museum**★★. Besides housing a sterling historical collection, this building is the nerve center for San Francisco's unique cable car network. A balcony walkway through the powerhouse features instructive panels that explain the system's operation.

Left: These 14ft (4m) winding wheels haul the 56 000ft (17 070m) of cable which run the city's cable cars (Cable Car Museum).

Right: Exhibits in the Diego Rivera Gallery, San Francisco Art Institute.

Lombard Street climbs Russian Hill, ending in a series of hairpin bends.

Russian Hill★

Hop aboard the Powell-Mason Line cable car at the museum and ride four blocks north to Russian Hill (the city's steepest). A 19C bohemian enclave, Russian Hill has remained a middle-class community with Edwardian homes, pueblo-style stucco houses and Art Deco apartment towers.

Enjoy the views from lush **Ina Coolbrith Park**, named after a late 19C-early 20C patroness of the arts (and Californian poet laureate). Nearby are numerous fine early 20C homes in the Arts and Crafts style. Especially note the seven-story **Williams-Polk House★** (1013 Vallejo St), built in 1892 and recently renovated.

Near the foot of Russian Hill is the **San Francisco Art Institute★** (800 Chestnut St), a prestigious fine-arts college founded in 1871, now housed in a 1926 hacienda-style building.

Its art exhibits and chapel-like Diego Rivera Gallery are open to the public.

The institute is a block north and east of that section of **Lombard Street★★★** known as 'the crookedest street in the world.' Falling from Hyde St to Leavenworth St, this avenue was cobbled in 1922 and its natural 27% grade reduced to 16% by the construction of eight hairpin bends. Banks of hydrangeas landscape the oft-photographed block; roughly three-quarters of a million cars negotiate its hairpin curves each year.

Fisherman's Wharf★★★

From the apex of Lombard, board the northbound Powell-Mason Line cable car and

Your first cable car ride – perhaps from the very top of town down to Fisherman's Wharf – is more thrilling than any roller coaster!

Trading wheat for coal and whiskey, the Balclutha *sailed twice a year between Britain and California (National Maritime Museum).*

descend five blocks to its Fisherman's Wharf terminus.

As the city's most popular tourist attraction, Fisherman's Wharf marries a maritime legacy to commercial kitsch. Working fishing boats, historic sailing ships and a pod of vociferous sea lions share the shoreline with converted piers and factories that extend from Fort Mason to Telegraph Hill. A carnival atmosphere prevails along Jefferson St, where buskers vie for space with seafood sellers and souvenir stands, side-by-side with novelty museums. Wharfside seafood restaurants, while perhaps not offering the city's finest cuisine, provide a fun-filled and scenic setting for dinner.

Above: Shall we dance? Impromptu dancing to a street band on Pier 41, Fisherman's Wharf.

Left: Crab vendor on Fisherman's Wharf.

Begin your exploration at the **National Maritime Museum★**, on the Aquatic Park Beach front just west of the cable car terminus. The museum occupies a 1939 Streamline Moderne building that resembles an ocean liner at berth. Its collection focuses on San Francisco's earliest years as a US port and contains many maritime artifacts; a separate exhibit shows steam vessels from the Civil War to modern times.

A third-floor observation deck overlooks **Hyde Street Pier**★★, which together with the museum comprises **San Francisco Maritime National Historical Park**. Its fleet of historic turn-of-the-20C ships may be the largest still afloat. Walk out the long wooden pier at the head of Powell St to see the six ships, five of which may be boarded and explored.

Most impressive of the quintet is the **Balclutha**★★, a three-masted, 301ft (92m), steel-hulled square-rigger launched in Glasgow in 1886. It sailed 17 times between California and Europe before being reassigned in 1904 to salmon-industry runs between Alaska and California. Also take a close look at the **Eureka**★, a sidewheel ferry that carried as many as 2 300 commuters; the **C A Thayer**★, a three-masted wooden schooner built to haul fir logs from Washington to California; and the steel-hulled steam tug **Hercules**, which towed railroad barges for more than a half century.

Nearby is **Ghirardelli Square**★★, a landmark shopping and dining complex. The original Ghirardelli Chocolate Factory, with its famous electric sign and clock tower, opened here in 1892. When the company moved operations to the East Bay in 1962, the old factory was redesigned. Today, exposed brick walls, hardwood floors and obsolete chocolate-making machinery recall industrial origins, although upscale galleries, boutiques and restaurants occupy the buildings.

Two blocks east is another historic reclamation project, **The Cannery**★★. Built in 1907, it once housed the most productive peach-canning operation in the world. On its third floor is the **Museum of the City of San Francisco**, whose collection includes photos and memorabilia from the city's history, including the great 1906 earthquake and fire.

Several dozen boats at moorage comprise

the city's colorful **fishing fleet**★. The vessels'
Italian names bear witness to the local fishing
heritage. The boats leave early in the morning
to fish for sole, cod, herring, sea bass, mackerel
and sand dab in the waters outside the Golden
Gate. Morning visitors are rewarded with the
sight of fishermen returning to unload their
catches. Twenty million pounds of seafood
come into this port annually.

The **USS Pampanito**★★ docks on the right
side of Pier 45. During two years of Pacific
service during the Second World War, this
deep-diving submarine sank six Japanese ships
and crippled four others. Its greatest fame
came in rescuing 73 prisoners of war from a
convoy that the Pampanito and two other

*A day's work done,
and all before lunch
– the fishing fleet at
Fisherman's Wharf.*

Alcatraz***

A mere 1.5 miles (2.4km) from Fisherman's Wharf, this infamous 12-acre (5ha) island once held scores of prisoners. Now inhabited mainly by scores of seabirds who nest among its crumbling ruins, 'The Rock', as it is aptly nicknamed, continues to exude a sense of foreboding. The cold, treacherous currents of San Francisco Bay swirl around its precipitous shore-line, while the perimeter of the island is a gnarl of coyote brush and blackberry brambles. A visit to Alcatraz is a haunting journey into a harsh chapter in American judicial history.

Named by 18C Spanish explorers because its nesting cormorants reminded them of the gannets – *alcatraces* – of their homeland, Alcatraz was unoccupied until the US established a garrison here in 1853. Regular troops deserted the island in 1907 and it became a full-time military prison until 1933, when it was transferred to the Department of Justice.

For the next three decades, Alcatraz was a maximum-security federal penitentiary reserved for 'public enemies' and other 'desperate and irredeemable criminals.' Its guard-to-prisoner ratio (1:3), brutal isolation cells and near-impenetrable security system nurtured its bleak reputation. Not one of the 36 prisoners who tried to escape the island is known to have succeeded.

In 1963, however, increasing maintenance costs and concerns by San Franciscans about the prison's proximity to their city hastened its closure. The National Park Service assumed control of the island in 1972 and designated it part of the Golden Gate National Recreation Area.

Ferries depart every 30 to 45 minutes from Pier 41 for the 15-minute cruise to Alcatraz. (It's wise to buy your tickets in advance.) Rangers meet the boats and provide an informative orientation before directing visitors to the exhibit area of the 1867 Barracks Building for a 12-minute video presentation. Then you're free to wander the island on your own.

One of the highlights is the forbidding **Cellhouse****. Built by the convicts themselves in 1911, it was (for a time) the largest reinforced concrete structure in the world. Enter near the bunker-like control center, formerly an arsenal of arms and tear gas. Beyond lies a visiting area where prisoners were separated from friends and family by thick plate glass, and spoke over monitored phones.

Once inside the cavernous main room, you can stroll down 'Broadway', a wide central passage between B and C blocks (leading to 'Times Square'), and step into a cramped, cold cell furnished with a regulation army cot, a folding table and chair, and a squat, open toilet. Prisoners who violated the strict rules of Alcatraz were subjected to solitary confinement in the dank isolation rooms, the 'dark holes', of D Block. Access to the recreation yard and library was a reward for good behavior.

The Cellhouse, home to notorious criminals such as Machine Gun Kelly and Al Capone.

submarines had jointly attacked. A haunting, self-guided audio tour leads through the sub's narrow corridors and small hatches.

Narrated **bay cruises★** depart from piers east of here. The Blue and Gold Fleet and the Red and White Fleet travel west along the shoreline, circle beneath the Golden Gate and pass by Alcatraz on their return. Both offer a different perspective on the city's hills, skyline and waterfront. Pier 41 is the departure point for boats to the island of **Alcatraz★★★** (*see* p.36).

Built over a dilapidated turn-of-the-century pier is **Pier 39★**, a festive, two-level marketplace of shops and amusements. Historic preservationists saved the pier in 1978. Tenants now include restaurants, a brightly painted carousel and an IMAX cinema. **Underwater World★** invites visitors to view marine life in a 300ft (91m) **tunnel★** through two aquarium tanks. The raucous barking of wild California **sea lions★**, who maintain residence on docks off Pier 39's west side, can be heard from as far as Telegraph Hill.

Left: Pier 39, with its resident sea lions, is a popular tourist attraction.

View over North Beach area to Fisherman's Wharf, from Coit Tower.

North Beach★★

Eight blocks south of Fisherman's Wharf is North Beach, erstwhile heart of the city's Italian community. Though North Beach has become far more ethnically diverse in recent years, the flavors and aromas of Little Italy still predominate in well-patronized trattorias, cafés and delicatessens.

This once was San Francisco's north-eastern shoreline. But as early as the 1850s land-hungry speculators began filling the bay's shallows and erecting an industrial zone. Italian immigration boomed from the 1880s to the early 1900s. By the 1950s, many Italian Americans had moved from North Beach; low rents attracted poor and disillusioned writers and artists who rejected social and artistic norms. Calling themselves the Beat Generation, the new bohemians smoked marijuana, listened to jazz and read verse.

Of their favorite haunts, few remain. **Caffe Trieste** (601 Vallejo St) was the place for espresso, while the **Vesuvio Cafe** (255 Columbus Ave) served endless glasses of red wine. When Beat poet Lawrence Ferlinghetti opened **City Lights Bookstore★** (261 Columbus Ave), opposite the Vesuvio in 1953, it was the first all-paperback bookstore in the US.

Columbus Avenue is the main thoroughfare of North Beach. Cutting diagonally across the normal grid of San Francisco streets, it was designed in 1872 to link the Financial District with Fisherman's Wharf. **Washington Square Park★** is roughly halfway along its course; the pentagonal plaza, with its broad lawn and clusters of willow, cypress and sycamore, is so tranquil that devotees of *t'ai chi chu'an* practise their graceful form of martial arts here each morning. Facing it is **SS Peter and Paul Church★**, a 1924 Gothic Revival-style church that offers Mass in English, Italian and Cantonese.

A three-block walk east brings you to the foot of **Telegraph Hill★**, named for a flag-signal system built on its 274ft (84m) summit in 1849 to announce the arrival of ships through the Golden Gate. **Coit Tower★★★**, one of the city's best-known landmarks, rises from a hilltop park. Erected in 1934 to honor city firefighters, the concrete column soars 212ft (65m). Take an elevator and a short flight of stairs to reach the observation deck atop the Tower. Sweeping **views★★★** take in downtown San Francisco, Marin County and the Golden Gate Bridge, the Bay Bridge and East Bay hills.

Coit Tower's public opening was delayed by a heated social controversy incited by 19 Depression-era murals in its lobby. The

The landmark Coit Tower, on Telegraph Hill, is home to a series of controversial murals which delayed its opening.

frescoes, created by 26 local artists over five months, depicted California life in the 1930s. But while celebrating the state's abundance and diversity, many works also bluntly criticized economic inequities during the Depression. After vigorous debate, and removal of blatant symbols of left-wing sympathy, the Tower finally opened to the public in 1934.

Instead of retracing your steps, descend the east side of Telegraph Hill to The Embarcadero via the **Filbert Steps★★**. These concrete and wooden stairs hide the lushly landscaped terraces of a hillside residential district. If you're a Humphrey Bogart fan, note the Art Deco apartment house at 1360 Montgomery St; it was featured in the 1947 film *Dark Passage*.

The Embarcadero★

Stretching to China Basin from Fisherman's Wharf, this 3 mile (5km) waterfront boulevard is one of the city's most vibrant, newly emerging public places. From Herb Caen Way …, a promenade that runs its length, you can enjoy views across the bay while inspecting outdoor art and 1990s architecture in renovated office and residential complexes.

The Embarcadero was built on landfill during the Gold Rush. Cross-bay ferries were docking here before the turn of the century, and daily commuter traffic swarmed through until the Bay Bridge opened in 1936. Construction of an elevated viaduct to link the Bay Bridge with the Golden Gate was halted by public outcry in 1959, but the unfinished roadway cast a massive shadow upon the waterfront until the 1989 Loma Prieta earthquake gave the city a reason to demolish it. Revitalization began soon after. Today, ongoing development – a streetcar line between Market Street and Fisherman's Wharf is nearing completion, and a new baseball stadium will open at China Basin in 2000 – defines this historic area.

Herb Caen Way …★ is the thread that binds the district. Named after a popular late *San Francisco Chronicle* columnist whose style was defined by the use of ellipses, the promenade is a favorite with joggers, bicyclists and in-line skaters.

The **Ferry Building★★**, at the head of Market St, was San Francisco's signature structure before the Golden Gate Bridge was constructed. Built of sandstone in 1898 and anchored on steel-framed concrete piers, it survived the 1906 quake with only its exterior stones loosened. Its tall clocktower, modeled on the Cathedral of Seville, still keeps accurate time. Today it contains the **World Trade Center**

and **International Children's Art Museum**.

Moored down the bayshore at Pier 32 is the **SS Jeremiah O'Brien★**, a Second World War survivor. The Liberty Ship, launched in June 1943, was part of the 5 000-ship armada that stormed Normandy Beach on D-Day 1944. Self-guided tours take in the wheelhouse, engine room, crew's quarters, deckside guns and ship's store. All-day cruises are offered several times a year.

The **San Francisco-Oakland Bay Bridge★★** begins its twin-spanned transit of the bay across piers 24 and 26. Yerba Buena Island, located mid-bay, is the rocky fulcrum for the 8.4 mile (13.5km) bridge, constructed between 1933 and 1936 (with a $77 million federal loan) to alleviate traffic on the transbay ferries. Overshadowed by the celebrity of the Golden Gate Bridge, which is less than one-fifth its length, this double-deck engineering marvel is a distinctive landmark in its own right.

The Bay Bridge actually is two spans

Linking the city with Oakland, the Bay Bridge took three years to construct.

connected by a tunnel through Yerba Buena Island. Between San Francisco and the island, a pair of 2 310ft (704m) suspension bridges are anchored by a concrete pier that rises 48 levels from the floor of the bay. Between the island and Oakland, the bridge is of cantilever design, a network of steel-and-concrete piers supporting the highway. Five lanes of traffic travel westbound on the upper deck, eastbound on the lower.

Financial District★★

Begin a walking tour of the city's Financial District at **Embarcadero Center★**, the largest office and commercial complex in San Francisco. A 10-acre (4ha) quartet of slab-like office towers facing the Ferry Building, it was built in 1982. The Center features three levels of shops with pedestrian bridges traversing cross-streets to link the four structures. A skydeck offers sweeping **views** from the 41st floor of the west tower (One Embarcadero Center).

Workers and shoppers take a break in the open areas around the Embarcadero Center buildings.

Across Market St is the **Federal Reserve Bank of San Francisco**, worth visiting to play the computer simulators in its lobby. Interactive programs teach basic economics: you can adjust the rate of money growth, set interest rates or raise and lower taxes, then gauge the effect on the economy. A new exhibit showcases American currency from colonial times to the present.

San Francisco's grandest bank building today houses the **Union Bank of California★★** (400 California St). Built in 1907, this temple to commerce exemplifies the energy and resources dedicated to rebuilding the city after the big quake. From the main banking hall, stairs lead down to the **Museum of Money of the American West**.

The **Transamerica Pyramid★★** (600 Montgomery St) is a leading symbol of modern San Francisco. The elegant 48-floor spire, completed in 1972, is the city's tallest building, rising 853ft (260m) from street level to the tip of its hollow lantern. Although the public is barred from its upper floors, a lobby-level 'virtual observation deck' offers **views** in four directions by means of rooftop monitors. An adjacent gallery displays contemporary art and design.

On the north side of the Pyramid is **Jackson Square★★**, the city's oldest surviving commercial neighborhood. Neither a 'square' nor a park, these four blocks of well-preserved

The distinctive Transamerica Pyramid has special design features to reduce the amount of shadow cast.

mid-19C structures once were the heart of the notorious Barbary Coast district. The two- and three-floor brick structures, some with cast-iron or stucco façades, outlasted the disaster of 1906; since the 1960s many have been converted into upscale art galleries and antique stores, design firms and law offices.

Two blocks south of the Pyramid is the **Wells Fargo History Museum★** (420 Montgomery St). The company played an integral part in the history of California, transporting gold and passengers by stagecoach as early as 1852, and this two-level museum tells its lively story. Gold assaying, the telegraph, stagecoach robberies and other subjects are portrayed; there are exhibits of photographs, documents, gold nuggets, bank notes and coins.

The **Bank of America Center★★** (555 California St) competes for dominance of the skyline with the Pyramid. Built in 1971, the

Take tea in the Garden Court, Palace Hotel, whose former patrons included Oscar Wilde, Rudyard Kipling and Sarah Bernhardt.

52-story granite-faced behemoth, 780ft (238m) high, takes up nearly an entire block. There are fine views from the top-floor lounge and restaurant. From the building's broad plaza, gaze north at the post-Modern design of **580 California Street**, incorporating 11 faceless, hooded human figures eerily encircling the 20th floor.

The **Pacific Exchange★** (301 Pine St), built in 1915, is notable for two massive Social Realist-style monuments that flank its entrance. Other buildings include **130 Bush Street** (1910), ten floors high but only 20ft (6m) wide; the 1927 **Hunter-Dulin Building★** (111 Sutter St), known as the office address of Sam Spade, Dashiell Hammett's fictional detective; and the 1917 **Hallidie Building★★** (130-150 Sutter St), a seven-floor office block considered the world's first glass curtain-walled structure.

Cross Market St to the **Palace Hotel★★**. Constructed in 1875, the Palace was the most opulent hotel in the West until gutted in 1906. Its owners immediately rebuilt it and the new Palace became the focal point of San Francisco's high society, hosting such luminaries as seven US presidents (Warren G Harding died here in 1923). It underwent complete restoration from 1989 to 1991, and again ranks among the city's top hotels.

Stroll down the main corridor to the **Garden Court★★**, capped by a stunning canopy of intricately leaded art glass. Once a courtyard where passengers stepped down from horse-drawn carriages, the room was transformed in 1909 into an indoor plaza where socialites joined dignitaries sipping tea and champagne beneath palm trees. Also worth seeing is **Maxfield's**, an elegant bar featuring an allegorical mural of the Pied Piper of Hamelin by Maxfield Parrish, and glass cases displaying memorabilia from the hotel's past.

South of Market★★

Follow 3rd St into the South of Market (SoMa) neighborhood. An area in transition from industrial to cultural, SoMa is caught in the purgatory between hardscrabble and high-tech. Like New York City's SoHo, the quarter is dominated by factory and warehouse structures, yet it pulses with some of San Francisco's most vibrant cultural activity.

Several renowned art museums and galleries make their homes in and around Yerba Buena Gardens along 3rd and 4th Sts, along with a huge convention center and a burgeoning multimedia industry. Development constraints in the Financial District have brought new office towers to SoMa's north-east corner, where former industrial buildings are reborn as spacious restaurants, lounges and theaters. Below 8th St, especially around 11th and Folsom Sts, there are many ultrahip nightclubs. Artists, designers, architects and filmmakers make their homes in SoMa's lofts, new apartments and condominiums.

As you walk south along 3rd, the new **San Francisco Museum of Modern Art★★**, or MOMA (*see* p.50), is the first notable building you may see. A short block to the west of the museum, on Mission St, are the offices of the **California Historical Society★**. In its first-floor galleries, visitors can explore the thematic exhibits illustrating the state's colorful past.

Directly behind MOMA on New Montgomery St is the **Pacific Telephone Building★** (1925). The 30-floor skyscraper boasts an elegant terracotta façade and arched brass doorways, and contains the **Pacific Bell Museum** of telephone history.

Cross 3rd from the museum to enter **Yerba Buena Gardens★★**. Its **Center for the Arts**, a low-slung 1993 building that resembles an ocean liner, contains three galleries (one

Like a phoenix from the ashes – the Yerba Buena Gardens complex has been created in a formerly depressed area.

devoted to multimedia presentations) and a theater. Exhibitions mix the work of culturally diverse, emerging Bay Area artists with those of world renown. At Yerba Buena's core is a 5.5-acre (2.2ha) **Esplanade**, its gently rolling hills, trees, gardens, eclectic sculptures and outdoor performance area providing a quiet green refuge.

A skybridge over Howard St leads to the **Moscone Convention Center**. Newly opened at its north-west corner is the $56 million **Rooftop Children's Center**, with an interactive museum, art studio and theater surrounding a central garden along with an ice rink, bowling alley, carousel and day-care center. Also

nearing completion is Sony's **Metreon**, a giant 'urban entertainment complex' whose attractions will include a 15-screen cinema and IMAX theater.

Opposite the Moscone Center on 4th St is the **Ansel Adams Center★**. Tucked into a converted industrial building, this award-winning museum exhibits historic and contemporary photographs and works in other visual media. It was named after San Francisco-born Adams (1902-1984), whose dramatic landscape photos of the American West brought new-found respect to photography as an art form. Adams fused his passion for social justice and environmental preservation with a desire to bring photography into the greater artistic community. One of the museum's five galleries is dedicated to his life and work.

Return up 4th St in the direction of Market and turn left to 814 Mission St: the **Cartoon Art Museum** is on the second floor of the old *Call-Bulletin* newspaper building. Since 1984 the museum has amassed an 11 000-piece collection dating from the late 18C. Rotating exhibits feature local and international cartoonists.

At 5th and Mission is the **Old Mint**. Though not open to the public, this 1874 structure is one of the city's finest neo-classical buildings. It served as a US Mint from 1874 to 1937; its $200 million in silver and gold narrowly escaped the fire of 1906. The stone-faced, brick building features six Doric columns and a pyramidal granite staircase to its grand entrance.

San Francisco Museum of Modern Art★★

San Francisco's premier showcase for contemporary art, the Museum of Modern Art (popularly known as MOMA), moved into an innovative new building in SoMa, facing Yerba Buena Gardens, in January 1995. After being lodged for six decades in the War Memorial Veterans Building at Civic Center, it now offers a striking addition to the city's skyline as well as to its cultural life.

Since its founding in 1871, the museum has had a long reputation for groundbreaking exhibitions, among them the first solo displays of works by then-unknown artists Clyfford Still, Jackson Pollock, Robert Motherwell and Mark Rothko. It still offers more than 70 shows a year highlighting pivotal movements and seminal works of American and international contemporary art.

The stunning atrium of the San Francisco Museum of Modern Art.

Swiss architect Mario Botta, known for his humanistic modernism and skilful use of natural light, was commissioned to design the space – his first building in the US and his first museum.

It is a striking composition of symmetrically arranged, stepped-back masses. Fine brickwork creates a rhythmic play of light and shadow across its exterior. Piercing the center of the building is a massive shaft, set off from the red-brown brick by stripes of alternating black and white stone. The top of the cylinder, which is faced with glass, slants toward 3rd St, creating a huge skylight that at once announces the museum's presence in the cityscape while suffusing the building's upper galleries and atrium with natural light. The museum's interior street level is plaza-like. The stunning central **atrium**★★ leads to a stylish café, a bookstore and a 299-seat theater.

The permanent collection, numbering more than 17 000 works of art, was initiated in 1935. Contemporary painting and sculpture has significant strengths in early Modernism and works by California and Bay Area artists. Photography (including gifts of works by Alfred Stieglitz, Ansel Adams and Imogen Cunningham), architecture and design, and media arts (video, film and computer-processed imagery) are other important collections.

Works drawn from the permanent collection occupy galleries on the second floor. Though these are frequently rotated, this is where visitors are likely to see mainstays of the painting collection such as Henri Matisse's *Femme au Chapeau*, a 1905 landmark of Fauvism; Georges Braque's *Violin and Candlestick* (1910), created during the height of Cubism; a selection of 100 works by Swiss artist Paul Klee; Mexican muralist Diego Rivera's sympathetically idealized *The Flower Carrier* (1935); and self-taught artist Frida Kahlo's perceptive detailed portrait of herself and her husband, *Frieda and Diego Rivera* (1931).

CENTRAL AND NORTHERN NEIGHBORHOODS

Contained within the triangle drawn by Market St and Golden Gate Ave, San Francisco's center of government occupies one of the finest groups of Beaux-Arts-style buildings in the US.

Civic Center★
Though the Civic Center suffers from proximity to the downtrodden Tenderloin district, the complex still reflects tenets of the early 20C 'City Beautiful' urban planning movement.

Construction of the Civic Center began in

1913 and continued for two decades. City Hall and the Civic Auditorium were opened in 1915, followed by a library and federal office buildings. The Veterans Building and the War Memorial Opera House were finished in 1932. The eyes of the world focused here in April-June 1945 when the United Nations Conference on International Organization convened in the Opera House. On 26 June, the UN Charter was signed in the Herbst Theatre of the Veterans Building.

Taking a break at the United Nations Plaza, Civic Center.

Completion in 1980 of Davies Symphony Hall as home for the city's orchestra expanded the Civic Center's role as a cultural center. The 1996 opening of a new Main Library and further plans for moving the Asian Art Museum to the old library brings hope for reducing some of the urban tarnish that afflicts the area.

Gateway to the Civic Center is the modern **United Nations Plaza★**, bordered by parallel rows of square columns carved with the names of UN member countries and the years in which they joined.

The high-tech **San Francisco Public Library★** showcases a modern take on classical Beaux-Arts design. The interior boasts a skylit atrium; changing exhibits are presented in the Jewett Gallery on the lower level. The old library, facing the new one to the north, is scheduled to house the Asian Art Museum by 2001.

Many consider **City Hall★★**, on Civic Center Plaza, to be San Francisco's most beautiful building. A massive edifice crowned by a magnificent dome that rises 307ft (94m) – higher than the US Capitol in Washington, DC – the four-floor structure takes up two city

blocks. Atlas-like figures support its west entrance, while Doric colonnades line its porticoes, façades and dome. Inside, a grand ceremonial staircase ascends to an open rotunda flanked by city government offices.

Built in Beaux-Arts style, City Hall is considered by many to be the city's most beautiful building.

Across Van Ness Ave stand the **San Francisco War Memorial and Performing Arts Center★★**. Flanking a formal courtyard, these twin structures served for decades as the city's center for the arts. The **War Memorial Opera House**, which hosted the original UN plenary sessions, is home to the acclaimed San Francisco Opera and San Francisco Ballet; they perform in an elegantly appointed 3 176-seat auditorium. The Veterans Building houses the intimate **Herbst Theatre**.

South of the Opera House is the **Louise M Davies Symphony Hall★**. The modern structure features a curving glass façade that reveals the lobby areas of the 2 743-seat hall. A bronze Henry Moore sculpture stands at its entrance.

Japantown

Japantown is a subdued and orderly neighborhood compared to busy Chinatown, both architecturally and socially. Its tidy, six-block core, 0.6 miles (1km) north of the Civic Center, displays well-maintained Victorian houses alongside neat but simple modern buildings, many with stucco and half-timbered exteriors which evoke the traditional rural architecture of Japan.

The striking modern structure in white marble of St Mary's Cathedral can be seen from afar.

The hub of Japantown is **Japan Center**, a five-building complex of galleries, shops, restaurants, cinemas and the deluxe Miyako Hotel. Its 110ft (33m) **Peace Pagoda** rises in five copper-roofed concrete tiers above the plaza. Otherwise, the center's design is contemporary and bland. Look around, however, and you'll find a classical Japanese bathhouse (Kabuki Hot Spring) and headquarters for the Ikenobo Ikebana Society for flower arranging.

Somewhat more traditional in style is **Nihonmachi Mall**, across Post St from Japan Center. The cobbled lane evokes the atmosphere of a Japanese village with 'half-timbered' buildings.

Around the corner to the north-east, within four blocks of Japan Center on Laguna and Pine Sts, are several typically Japanese houses of worship. The **Sokoji-Soto Zen Buddhist Temple** is run by robed monks who chant at the foot of a golden image of the Buddha. The **Konko Church of San Francisco** incorporates an austere, natural-wood Shinto altar with Christian influences. The **Buddhist Church of San Francisco★**, which adheres to the Jodo

Shinshu (Pure Land) sect, is capped by a stupa containing a relic of the Buddha.

Immediately south-east of Japan Center is **St Mary's Cathedral★★**, the city's Roman Catholic cathedral. Sheathed in white travertine marble and visible from miles around, the striking 1971 structure sits atop gentle Cathedral Hill. Its most daring design attribute is a reinforced concrete cupola enclosing a soaring atrium. Narrow stained-glass windows rise spectacularly to meet at the cupola's apex, forming a brilliant cross 190ft (58m) above the sanctuary floor.

Haas-Lilienthal House, on Franklin Street, is one of the few Victorian-era residences open to the public.

Pacific Heights★★

Just north of Japantown, elite Pacific Heights' lively and unpretentious commercial district stretches along Fillmore St. Occupying an east-west ridge, Pacific Heights holds some of the city's finest houses and loveliest **views★★**, and offers a glimpse of the lives of affluent early-20C San Franciscans.

At its heart is **Alta Plaza Park**, a public park since the mid 1850s. The lush oasis features terraces that drop down its south side, forming a ziggurat of concrete and shrubbery opposite a row of 1875 Italianate-style Victorian houses, among the oldest in the city.

Five blocks east of Alta Plaza, on Washington St, is the ostentatious **Spreckels Mansion★★**. The French Baroque-style palace was built in 1913 for sugar magnate Adolph Spreckels, whose wife, Alma, was patroness of the California Palace of the Legion of Honor. Two blocks further, on Franklin St, is the 1886 **Haas-Lilienthal House★★**, a Victorian residence open to the public (by one-hour guided tours on Wednesdays and Sundays). Several of the Queen Anne upper-floor rooms are furnished in 1880s-1920s decorative styles, while the basement displays period photos.

Cow Hollow

Wedged between Pacific Heights and the Marina District, Cow Hollow was once a dairy-farming district. The 'hollow' was replaced in the 1890s by wood-frame houses that survived the 1906 quake unscathed; they now host trendy shops and cafés along **Union St★**. Pedestrians wander through patios and courtyards, occasionally stumbling upon an evocative reminder of the rural past. The quiet lane known as **Charlton Court**, for instance, once served as a depot for milk wagons. The 1870 house and barn of dairyman James

Cudworth stand behind a palm tree on Union.

Union Street's best-known building is the 1861 **Octagon House★**, at the corner of Gough St. It was designed after a popular book claimed that octagonal houses provide more light, space and ventilation than normal square-cornered houses. The Colonial Dames of America use the house to display a collection of early American decorative arts including furniture, ceramics, pewter, silverware and portraits. In one room are documents handwritten by such Independence-era leaders as Thomas Jefferson and Benjamin Franklin.

Enjoy a stroll among the renovated Victorians of Union Street, many of which are now boutiques, galleries and craft shops.

Marina District★

After the 1906 quake, city boosters chose a marshy inlet on the city's northern waterfront as site of the Panama-Pacific International Exposition of 1915. The Army Corps of Engineers filled 635 acres (257ha) with sand and earthquake debris, creating a flat, attractive world's fair site. Architects designed a complex of wood-and-plaster pavilions for 25 countries and 29 states: a fantasy city of Renaissance palazzos, Spanish missions and Byzantine domes. When the fair ended, having drawn nearly 20 million visitors in 10 months, only the Palace of Fine Arts was saved from demolition.

Developers laid out residential streets and built choice homes on the landfill. The Marina became known as a desirable middle-class address. Ironically, when the Loma Prieta earthquake struck in 1989, the unstable ground beneath the Marina liquefied, causing several structures to collapse and heavily damaging dozens of other buildings.

Start a tour at **Fort Mason★**, west of Fisherman's Wharf. A US military reservation from 1850, this hill served as the Army's western command center during the late 19C Indian wars and as headquarters for the interim city government after the 1906 quake. Since 1972, Fort Mason has been part of the **Golden Gate National Recreation Area (GGNRA)**. The GGNRA Headquarters and visitor center are in a turn-of-the-century Army hospital.

On the bayshore is **Fort Mason Center★**, a set of warehouses, barracks and docks that served from 1910 to 1962 as the main departure point for Americans in Pacific wars, but now have been transformed into a community cultural complex.

Building E, easternmost of the former barracks, houses the **J Porter Shaw Library**, operated by the San Francisco Maritime National Historical Park. Building D is home to the **Mexican Museum★**, which is planning to move to SoMa about 2000; it features pre-Spanish, Colonial and modern arts of Mexico and the Hispanic US, among them Mayan and Aztec artifacts, folk arts, jewelry and masks.

Building C houses two museums: the **San Francisco African American Historical & Cultural Society** and **Museo ItaloAmericano**. Both mount exhibits of ethnic art and history and offer community education programs.

In Building A you'll find the **San Francisco Craft & Folk Art Museum**, which exhibits historical folk art and contemporary crafts from around the world. At the end of Pier 2, the **Cowell Theater** is built over the water beyond the Herbst Pavilion.

The thread that binds the Marina District is **Golden Gate Promenade**, a pedestrian and bike path that runs 3.5 miles (5.6km) from Aquatic Park to the Golden Gate Bridge. West of Fort Mason, it skirts **Marina Green**, a 10-acre (4ha) greensward popular for its kite-flying breezes and its views of San Francisco Bay.

The **Palace of Fine Arts★★** is just south and west of the Marina Yacht Harbor. The rotunda and peristyle, among San Francisco's best-known landmarks, were designed to house art for the 1915 fair. But the original building, inspired by an 18C engraving and a 19C painting of a royal tomb, was never intended to be permanent. Not until the 1960s was the building reconstructed in concrete and steel.

The Palace projects a sense of mystery and melancholy. The rotunda, 110ft (35m) high and 135ft (43m) across, is decorated with bas-relief panels. Angels look down from the interior of the dome, while female figures sculpted along the top face inward, their faces buried in their arms. On clear, calm days, the large pond spreading from the eastern foot of the rotunda reflects mirror images.

The grandiose rotunda and peristyle of the Palace of Fine Arts are built on the romantic designs of Bernard Maybeck.

Located behind the rotunda is the **Exploratorium**★★, an interactive museum of science, art and human perception. More than 650 'hands-on' exhibits in physics, electricity, life sciences, weather, light, psychology, sense perception and other subjects enlighten children and adults alike.

The Presidio★★

For more than two centuries after its 1776 establishment, its privileged setting on 1 480 forested acres (599ha) above the Golden Gate earned the Presidio a reputation as the most beautiful military installation in North America. Although its original Spanish landlords gave it only minimal attention despite its strategic location, the fort was restored and enlarged after California was ceded to the US. The protection of Sierra gold and silver made defense of San Francisco Bay a top Union priority during the Civil War. Later, Presidio troops helped maintain order in the city and hosted more than 16 000 refugees who camped on its open lands after the 1906 quake.

Millions of US troops trained here for combat during the world wars. The base subsequently was a command center for Nike missile defense of the bay and headquarters for the Sixth US Army until 1994, when troops marched off the grounds for the last time. The Presidio now is part of the Golden Gate National Recreation Area.

Enter its grounds via the Lombard Gate, three blocks from the Palace of Fine Arts. Signs direct you west to the **Main Post**★★, focal point of activity on the former base. Start at the **Visitor Center**, with the GGNRA offices in the stately brick barracks (1890). Follow the edge of the Parade Ground to the **Presidio Museum**★, with its dioramas and photos from the 1906 quake and the 1915 Panama-Pacific Exposition.

Golden Gate Bridge***

Stretching across a narrow strait, above the swirling union of the Pacific Ocean and San Francisco Bay, this orange vermilion, Art Deco suspension bridge is one of San Francisco's most beloved symbols.

Imagined by a madman in 1869, proposed intermittently over the next four decades by saner visionaries, the bridge elicited resistance and emotions at every stage of its conception. Few took the idea seriously until 1916, when motor vehicles were becoming a way of life. Initial cost estimates ran as high as $100 million, but Joseph Strauss, a tireless and innovative engineer who had built more than 400 bridges around the world, claimed he could span the 'unspannable' passage for a mere $27 million.

Citizens from San Francisco to the Oregon border pledged financial and political support. But there was strong opposition from the Southern Pacific Railroad, sole owner of all transbay ferry operations, and the US War Department, which feared the bridge would hinder navigation and provide a target in the event of a war. When opposition was finally retracted, the Great Depression had crushed the economy. Only when A P Giannini, founder of the Bank of Italy, declared his bank would finance the project did it proceed in 1933.

Bridge construction offered steady employment for thousands in the Depression, and Strauss enforced such new safety measures as safety belts, nets and filter glasses to block the blinding sun. Only two fatal accidents occurred during construction – although the latter incident, three months before completion, took ten lives.

When the bridge opened on 27 May 1937, it was hailed as a model of safety, economy and grace. The final cost of $35 million was more than Strauss' 1921 estimate, but far less than many had predicted. Today, nearly 130 000 vehicles traverse the bridge daily, and pedestrians take to its sidewalks to admire soaring towers, graceful cables and wondrous views.

Measuring 1.22 miles (1.98km), not including approaches, the Golden Gate was the world's longest suspension bridge until superseded in 1964 by New York's Verrazano Narrows Bridge.

A suspension bridge relies on gravity for stability. The weight of the roadway, suspended from cables anchored on land, keeps it from falling. Cables provide flexibility for the midspan of the bridge to deflect up to 27ft (8.4m) in high winds without jeopardizing structural integrity.

There are five main components. At the Golden Gate, two **piers** form the bases of the towers, while concrete-block **anchorages** support the bridge at either end. Twin steel **towers** rise 746ft (227m, 65 stories) above the piers, and each supports a total load of 61 500 tons (56 000 tonnes) from the two main **cables**. Spun out of 80 000 miles (128 000km) of wire, these cables rest in saddles atop the towers and are embedded into the anchorages on land. The steel-reinforced **roadway** hangs from ropes attached to the cables at 50ft (16m) intervals.

Continue down tree-lined **Officers Row★** to **Pershing Square**, where stood the home of General John 'Black Jack' Pershing, a First World War hero. A flagpole marks the corner of the original 1776 adobe compound.

The 28-acre (11ha) **San Francisco National Military Cemetery★** is reached off Sheridan St at Lincoln Blvd. Graves of veterans date from as far back as the Civil War. On the bayshore is **Crissy Field**, an aircraft test site from 1919 to 1936. Many original buildings still stand, including hangars that once held cloth biplanes. The area is now under development.

Tucked under the Golden Gate Bridge at the northern tip of the Presidio grounds is **Fort Point National Historic Site★★**. The brick-and-granite fortress was built in 1861 as a Civil War garrison. By 1885 its guns were removed for scrap and the fort was rarely occupied thereafter. Bridge builder Joseph Strauss, however, was so impressed by its masonry that

Fort Point National Historic Site is tucked beside the southern pier of the Golden Gate Bridge.

Whether it's cloaked in mist, or blazing against a faultless blue sky, you will always remember your first sighting of the legendary Golden Gate Bridge.

he designed a massive steel arch to preserve the structure. Restored by the Park Service in the 1970s, Fort Point today provides a glimpse into late-19C California military life. Exhibits detail the history of the fort and the lives of soldiers stationed there.

Presidio Heights

A casual stroll through this affluent neighborhood, immediately south of the Presidio, reveals a broad variety of architectural styles: Norman, Tudor, Italianate, Queen Anne, Romanesque. Especially worth noting is the **Roos House** (3500 Jackson St), a massive, half-timbered residence designed in 1909 by renowned Arts and Crafts architect Bernard Maybeck.

You can take a 30-minute guided tour of **Temple Emanu-El★**, at Arguello Blvd and Lake St. Built in 1926, the orange-tiled, Byzantine-style dome rises 150ft (49m) from the ground and is visible for miles. The vestibule ceiling is decorated with a brilliant blue and yellow fresco of a star-studded sky. At the altar, the sacred ark stands under a marble canopy, housed in a gilded bronze tabernacle box inlaid with cloisonné.

The **Swedenborgian Church★★** (2107 Lyon St) is a lovingly crafted wood-and-brick chapel in the Arts and Crafts style. It was conceived in 1895 by the Revd Joseph Worcester, a devotee of the writings of Swedish scientist-philosopher Emanuel Swedenborg. Worcester enlisted the help of talented friends, including architects Maybeck and Willis Polk, to create a church interior that replicates the natural beauty of a woodland.

The **San Francisco Fire Department Museum** (655 Presidio Ave) is also worth a visit. A converted firehouse garage, it houses many historic fire engines, including the city's first

Once a Jewish Cemetery, Mission Dolores Park is now a resting place for those seeking respite from the city.

hand-drawn pump cart (1849). Historical displays, photos and memorabilia include fire helmets, uniforms, hydrants and extinguishers.

SOUTHERN AND WESTERN NEIGHBORHOODS

Mission District★

San Francisco's birthplace was the Mission District. Mission San Francisco de Asis (Mission Dolores) was dedicated on 29 June 1776 and a primitive village grew up around it. Today it remains a largely Hispanic and working-class community. In its commercial heart – tree-lined **24th Street★** between Mission and Potrero Sts – salsa music blares from small shops, groceries, *taquerias* and restaurants. Stroll down **Balmy Alley★** (between Treat and Harrison Sts) to admire bold murals adorning nearly every garage door and wall surface.

The central landmark of the district, as it has been for well over two centuries, is **Mission Dolores★** (16th and Dolores Sts). San Francisco's oldest standing building is a distinct reminder of the city's Spanish heritage and a repository of early European history.

The chapel of Mission Dolores has been carefully restored.

Despite long periods of neglect in the 19C, its remarkably sturdy **chapel★★**, built in 1791, has survived several major earthquakes. Restored in 1995, it now appears much as it did when first built. Cement stucco covers 4ft-thick adobe walls, while amber-colored windows bathe the interior in warm light. The ornate hand-carved 18C reredos and side altars were imported from Mexico.

The lavishly ornamented mission **church** was built in 1918 and designated a basilica in 1952. A small **museum** houses shards of artifacts discovered during restoration, as well as colonial vestments. On the south side is a tranquil **cemetery★** where many of San Francisco's early leaders are buried.

Book ahead to join a 75-minute guided tour (Tue and Wed) of the **Levi Strauss & Company** (250 Valencia St). In 1873, German-born Strauss patented a design he developed while making overalls for miners during the Gold Rush. It included the now-famous back-pocket design and reinforced copper rivets.

Castro District

West of the Mission is the lively neighborhood that forms the heart of San Francisco's gay community. Bars, restaurants, trendy clothing stores and boutiques (with names like 'All American Boy' and 'Does Your Father Know') crowd together along Castro, Market and 18th Sts, while side streets are lined with beautifully refurbished townhouses known as Victorians.

Once a blue-collar neighborhood, the Castro assumed its current cosmopolitan mix in the 1960s and 1970s when gays began to buy homes here. The enclave became overt about its identity with social liberalization and the city's passage, in 1978, of the Gay Bill of Civil Rights, protecting gays from discrimination in housing and employment. The onset of the AIDS epidemic created a crisis in the 1980s, but Castro residents responded with public education and support groups.

An upbeat, neighborly attitude pervades the district. Walk down busy **Castro Street** between Market and 19th to take in the bookstores and bars, boutiques and tony cafés. Dance music pulses in many shops, and creative, sometimes outrageous, window displays are among the most eye-catching in the city. Along adjacent residential streets, rainbow flags symbolizing gay liberation brighten the windows of many homes.

The **Castro Theatre★** is the city's finest example of early-20C movie-palace architecture. Built in Spanish Renaissance Revival style in 1922, the two-floor, 1 450-seat theater boasts a curving green and gold-leaf ceiling and sumptuous murals on its walls. Outside, a huge pink neon sign brightens the low-hanging marquee. Foreign and classic films make up the bulk of its repertoire.

The **NAMES Project** occupies a storefront on adjacent Market St between Castro and Church

Sts. Called the 'largest community art project in the world,' it sponsors the AIDS Memorial Quilt. Composed of 3ft by 6ft (1m by 2m) panels, each handmade in memory of someone who has died of AIDS, the quilt tours the world to promote AIDS awareness. Visitors are welcome to step inside to view the panel storage areas and the small sewing workshop.

Haight-Ashbury

More than three decades have passed since the Summer of Love, but a countercultural ethos clings to Haight-Ashbury. Named after an intersection at its heart, the Haight draws hordes of young people to its parks and sidewalks, thrift (second-hand) stores and coffeehouses. Its Victorian homes, nestled between Golden Gate and Buena Vista parks, have attracted a steady influx of ambitious renovators since the mid-1970s.

At the turn of the 20C, the Haight blossomed into a countercultural

Haight-Ashbury has retained its colorful, eclectic community, and is still a magnet for the young and young-at-heart.

haven in the 1960s, celebrating rock music, mind-altering drugs and free love. An estimated 20 000 people crammed into Golden Gate Park in January 1967 for the Human Be-In, an anti-establishment celebration featuring poetry readings and rock concerts. Haight musicians, including Janis Joplin and the Grateful Dead (Jerry Garcia lived at 710 Ashbury St), invented the wandering, melodic San Francisco Sound that catapulted them to fame. In the ensuing 'Summer of Love', 75 000 'hippies' flocked to the neighbourhood, sleeping in the parks and attending free concerts and parties.

In 1968, many hippies left the Haight for rural communes and heroin replaced LSD and marijuana. In the 1980s the district re-emerged as a middle-class enclave, albeit with an anti-establishment heart. Disaffected youths today congregate on street corners with middle-aged denizens whose appearance seems only to have greyed since 1967.

Most of the Haight's Victorian townhouses are of the asymmetrical Queen Anne substyle. These were frequently built in rows of four or five, identical but for colors and decorative details. A stroll along Page, Central, Masonic or Waller Sts reveals many fanciful examples of these homes. But the San Francisco's best-known Victorians are several blocks north-east of the Haight, on Steiner St facing **Alamo Square**. Nicknamed 'Postcard Row', the seven houses stand before a snapshot-ready backdrop of the full downtown skyline. South of the Haight, the **Twin Peaks** ★★ dominate the city

Veteran Haight denizens.

The Alamo Square Victorians, understandably known as 'Postcard Row', must be one of the most photographed streets in San Francisco.

skyline. The distinct but adjacent peaks reach 904ft (276m) and 922ft (281m). Most visitors are content with the **panorama★★★** to the north and east from the parking area, though it is possible to climb the grassy slopes of either peak for a more distant view.

Golden Gate Park★★★

The largest cultivated urban park in the US, Golden Gate Park stretches 3 miles (4.8km) inland from Ocean Beach and encompasses more than 1 017 acres (412 ha) of meadows, gardens and public buildings. The park's 34.5 miles (56km) of trails link an enchantingly natural, yet entirely manmade, landscape of lakes and woods.

The park was built in the 1870s to rival New York's new Central Park. Engineers shielded the sandy site from ocean winds, graded inland dunes, planted and nurtured large trees where

The Conservatory of Flowers is sure to be a great attraction when it reopens after renovation.

there had been none, and laid out a meandering road system. Its shining light was Scotsman John McLaren, park superintendent from 1890 until his death in 1943. McLaren fought hard against new buildings, concessions and other urban intrusions as he planted millions of flowers, bulbs and trees.

In 1893, M H de Young, co-founder of *The San Francisco Chronicle* newspaper, persuaded city officials to mount a world fair at the park. Five domed and spired buildings, erected around a quadrangle called the Great Court, became the centerpiece of the California Midwinter International Exposition in 1894. Visitors still flock to the fair site, now the **Music Concourse**, to hear Sunday concerts in Spreckels Bandshell and to tour the M H de Young Memorial Museum, the Asian Art Museum, and the various components of the California Academy of Sciences. John F Kennedy Drive winds through the length of the park. At its east end is the

SOUTHERN & WESTERN NEIGHBORHOODS

Conservatory of Flowers★, scheduled to reopen in 2000 after extensive repair. The Victorian glass palace shelters more than 20 000 rare and exotic plants. Nearby are a spring-blooming rhododendron dell, a bower of giant tree ferns, and a playground featuring a magnificent 1912 **carousel**★.

In the central park is the 70-acre (28ha) **Strybing Arboretum**★★, whose collection comprises 6 000 species of plants from all over the world, especially regions of Mediterranean climate. Close by is the tranquil **Japanese Tea Garden**★★, which has a maze of winding paths, *bonsai*, ornamental ponds, a wooden pagoda, a Zen rock garden and a teahouse. In its midst is a 10.5ft (3.2m) Buddha image, cast in Japan in 1790 and the largest bronze Buddha outside Asia.

The Japanese Tea Garden is one of the most beautiful parts of Golden Gate Park.

Three outstanding museums surround the Music Concourse.

The M H de Young Memorial Museum★★, which opened in 1895 in the world fair's Egyptian Revival-style Fine Arts Building, has evolved into a mature art museum specializing in American fine and decorative arts from the pre-Columbian era to the present. Anchored by de Young's personal collection, the museum "took off" following an extraordinary bequest by John D Rockefeller III of 137 paintings and other American works. Donations by other benefactors provided extensive collections of indigenous African and Oceanic art, pre-Columbian art, Near Eastern and Central Asian tribal weavings and contemporary American printmaking.

Explore the de Young Museum by moving clockwise around the central, skylit Hearst Court. **American Art★★★** is displayed chronologically. The collection is outstanding in portrait, landscape, trompe-l'œil and genre painting and sculpture. A decorative-arts display presents 18C and 19C furnishings, including dining-room and parlor displays, as well as silver, glass and porcelain. African, Oceanic, ancient American and Textile collections are exhibited to the right of the entry hallway. **Arts of the Americas★** features objects from Mesoamerica and South America, circa 1200 BC to AD 1520, as well as murals from the ancient Mexican city of Teotihuacán.

The collection in the adjacent **Asian Art Museum★★★** is considered the finest in North America. Spawned by the collection of Avery Brundage (1887-1975), longtime head of the International Olympic Committee, the

Ming Dynasty Buddha from the Asian Art Museum, Golden Gate Park.

museum's 12 000 works include Chinese jades, ceramics, ritual bronzes and paintings from the Ming and Qing dynasties; the nation's most complete assemblage of Japanese art; significant holdings of Indian and Southeast Asian religious statuary; and Korean, Himalayan and Near Eastern artwork.

Brundage presented his collection to San Francisco in 1959 when the city pledged to build a museum to display it. The museum opened in 1966. However, with space to display only 12%-15% of the collection at any given time, it has outgrown its present home. A relocation (scheduled for the end of 2001) to the Old Library building at the Civic Center will provide more than three times the space.

Enter the Asian Art Museum through the Gruhn Court from the west side of the de Young Museum. The brilliant Treasure Wall, designed after a Qing dynasty treasure case in Beijing's Forbidden City, contains ceramics and carvings from throughout Asia and serves as an overview of collections.

The **Chinese Art★★★** collection, on the first floor, comprises more than half of the museum's holdings. Six thousand bronzes, sculptures, paintings and objects of decorative art exemplify the beauty and diversity of Chinese art since Neolithic times. Paintings and calligraphy emphasize the works of 15C-19C masters with huge landscapes and still-life scrolls.

The **Korean Art★** exhibit, also on the first floor, features hanging scrolls, stoneware ceramics, gold jewelry, ash-glazed funerary pottery and a broad collection of celadon-glazed vessels.

More than 4 200 works of **Japanese Art★★** include temple bronzes, ceramics, Buddhist scrolls, samurai swords and decorative arts. The museum also has a collection of *netsuke* (kimono fastener) miniatures in horn and ivory, an exhibit on the traditional tea ceremony, and calligraphy in different styles and formats from the 12C-20C.

The **Indian Art★** collection boasts a wealth of religious statues and carvings in stone, bronze, terracotta and wood representing sculptural styles from every school and period of Indian art from the 3C BC to AD 19C. **Tibet and the Himalayas★** places an emphasis on religious art, including the unique scroll paintings known as *thangkas*.

Southeast Asian Art★ comprises religious and decorative pieces from Indonesia, the Philippines, Malaysia, Thailand, Burma and Indochina (Vietnam, Laos and Cambodia).

Directly across the Music Concourse from the M H de Young and Asian Art museums is the **California Academy of Sciences★★**. Formed in 1853 in the wake of the Gold Rush, the Academy of Sciences began as a group of naturalists who collected specimens and presented scholarly papers. The oldest scientific institution in the West, it has three separate divisions: the Natural History Museum, one of the ten largest in the world, harboring more than 14 million specimens; the Steinhart Aquarium, oldest in the US; and the Morrison Planetarium, first planetarium to be constructed entirely in the US.

The highlight of the interactive **Natural History Museum★★** is 'Life Through Time', a challenging exhibit that traces evolutionary adaptations

Making friends with a sea lion statue is definitely a hands-on experience at the California Academy of Sciences.

of body structures over 3.5 billion years. An interactive computer program allows users to select a life form and explore its sequence of development, learning how all living things are interconnected and why certain forms are more closely related than others. Dioramas highlight wildlife in the varied ecosystems of California and the African savanna. There are displays on anthropology, geology and space exploration.

From the Earth and Space Hall, enter the **Morrison Planetarium★**, which produces a half-dozen new shows annually on such topics as astronomical discoveries, celestial navigation, and approaching comets, meteor showers and eclipses.

The 185 exhibits in the **Steinhart Aquarium★** feature sea creatures from around the globe. Walk clockwise around a crocodile-infested swamp to a darkened hall where fish glide and glimmer in lighted tanks. Past the breeding colony of penguins lies the Coral Reef, a community of coral plants and invertebrate animals. At the Fish Roundabout, stand at the center of a doughnut-shaped, 100 000-gallon tank to observe the schooling behavior of fast-swimming ocean fish.

Richmond District

One of San Francisco's most ethnically diverse neighborhoods, Richmond is a relatively flat expanse of undistinguished terraced houses sandwiched between Golden Gate Park and the Presidio. Always a multi-ethnic neighborhood, its most charming thoroughfare is **Clement Street**. Locals throng here for excellent yet understated restaurants that line the 12 blocks west from Arguello Blvd. The stretch is sometimes known as 'New Chinatown' because so many of its residents have relocated from downtown Chinatown since the 1970s.

East of Arguello, off Anza St, the **San Francisco Columbarium** is a copper-roofed, neo-classical rotunda that harkens to the days when cemeteries covered Richmond's shallow dunes. It holds more than 4 400 niches for cremated remains, including those of many prominent San Francisco families. The flamboyant interior is adorned with stained glass and brightly painted plaster filigree.

Sutro Heights

This rugged north-west corner of the city has drawn visitors to its rocky cliffs and sheltered coves since prehistoric Indians camped here. Now part of the Golden Gate National Recreation Area, it is an impressive natural refuge.

The first permanent structure was Seal Rock House, which drew city dwellers for beach outings in the mid-1850s. But the area did not boom until the 1880s, when Adolph Sutro, who made a fortune building a tunnel under Nevada's Comstock Lode, invested his millions in San Francisco real estate. One-twelfth of all city property soon belonged to the Prussian immigrant. His hugely popular Sutro Baths, lush estate on Sutro Heights, 5-cent railway and rebuilt Cliff House gave the oceanfront a reputation as a place of leisure for every economic class. In the 1920s and 1930s, an entertainment zone – featuring Playland-at-the-Beach amusement park – spread from here to Golden Gate Park.

The site of Sutro's estate is now encompassed by **Sutro Heights Park★** on a striking promontory overlooking Cliff House and Ocean Beach. Although the residence was demolished in 1939, the property remains a paradise of drought-resistant flowers and trees from all over the world. The **Sutro Baths★**, however, are survived only by concrete foundations and brackish pools in a rocky cove. Once covered by a three-floor glass dome, they comprised seven luxurious tidal pools of varying temperatures, served by 500 private dressing rooms, bleachers seating 5 300, and three restaurants.

The **Cliff House★** restaurant – third incarnation of an 1863 roadhouse – recalls the area's heyday. This 1909 version has been renovated and modernized several times. Visitors enjoy stunning views of Ocean Beach and glimpses of brown pelicans, cormorants and seals basking on the offshore Seal Rocks. A well-stocked visitor center on the lower deck offers GGNRA maps and information. On Cliff House's lower terrace is the **Musée Mécanique**, a gallery with an odd collection of antique amusements including coin-operated player pianos, mobile dioramas made entirely of toothpicks, and penny-arcade picture machines, many from Playland.

The **California Palace of the Legion of Honor★★** is just east of Sutro Heights. San Francisco's leading museum of European art,

Lost in thought – Rodin's The Thinker, *California Palace of the Legion of Honor.*

HONNEUR ET PATRIE

the Legion boasts one of the finest collections of Auguste Rodin sculptures outside Paris. Built in 1924 with a gift to the city from arts patroness Alma de Bretteville Spreckels, it enjoys a spectacular setting amid the cypresses of Lincoln Park. The building was modeled after Paris' 18C Palais de la Legion d'Honneur, and dedicated to the 3 600 Californians who perished in the First World War.

The original holdings were primarily dance-related art, European decorative arts and Spreckels' personal collection of works by the French sculptor Rodin. The Legion now owns 106 Rodin sculptures, of which the most famous, *The Thinker* (1880), greets visitors in the outdoor Court of Honor. A pyramidal skylight was added to the Court of Honor in 1995, offering homage to I M Pei's famed structure at the Louvre.

Arrayed with neo-classical symmetry around a central rotunda, the 19 main-floor galleries present a selective survey of European art (mainly Italian, French, British and Dutch) from medieval to modern times. You'll find works by Titian, Rubens, Gainsborough, and such acclaimed 19C-20C painters as Degas, Cezanne, Manet, Monet, Matisse and Picasso. Antiquities and porcelain are shown on the lower level, where the museum's bookstore, café and theater are also located. The Legion also displays selections from the Achenbach Foundation for Graphic Arts, a body of work that numbers 80 000 prints, drawings, photographs and illustrated books.

Sunset District

Covering the south-west quadrant of San Francisco below Golden Gate Park and west of Twin Peaks, the wind-scoured Sunset District comprises a broad grid of stucco row (terraced) houses of cookie-cutter sameness.

The district's leading point of interest is **Ocean Beach★**, a sandy seam between city and ocean. Pounding surf and a dangerous undertow make swimming unwise, though you may see schools of wet-suited surfers paddle out to await the perfect wave. A paved promenade extends 3 miles (4.8km) along the grassy dunes from Sloat Blvd to just south of Cliff House, appealing to bikers, joggers and in-line skaters.

The beach's southern end is fringed by a broad parkland surrounding Lake Merced, another popular recreation destination. Near its northern shore is the 125-acre (50ha) **San Francisco Zoo★**, home to nearly 1 000 animals of more than 260 species. Built in the 1930s, it has featured cageless, 'natural habitat' displays since the 1980s. The zoo currently is designing new habitats and expanding its facilities for breeding endangered species.

EXCURSIONS

Marin County

North of the Golden Gate extend 15sq miles (38km²) of pristine coastal lands known as the **Marin Headlands★★**. This remarkable preserve of windswept ridges, sheltered valleys, sandy coves and scattered vestiges of military history are protected as part of the Golden Gate National Recreation Area. Except when summer fogs roll over these hills, the headlands offer outstanding **views** of the city-fringed bay, Golden Gate Bridge elegantly overlapping the San Francisco skyline and the vast Pacific Ocean stretching away to the western horizon.

The area was once considered of key strategic importance;

Brown pelicans, just some of the wildife to be seen along the coastline of Marin County.

obsolete defense batteries and gun emplacements pockmark the landscape. Otherwise, the headlands are thickly covered with coastal grasses, sagebrush and oak woodlands – habitat for lizards and snakes, foxes and black-tailed deer. In spring, colorful wildflowers decorate the hillsides. Lagoons and coves attract stately egrets and herons, while fleets of brown pelicans patrol the coastal waters, and offshore rocks provide haven for seals, sea lions and nesting shorebirds.

There are no finer **views★★★** of San Francisco than from **Conzelman Road★★★**, reached by crossing the Golden Gate on US-101 and exiting at Alexander Avenue. The route snakes along the headlands' curvaceous bluffs. Beyond Hawk Hill, a key point on the West Coast flyway for migrating birds of prey, it crests and becomes a winding one-way passage down the precipitous edge of a high sea cliff.

A 0.5 mile (0.8km) trail leads to the **Point Bonita Lighthouse★**. Perched on a rocky promontory, this lighthouse has guided mariners through the Golden Gate since 1855. Automated in 1981 and restored in 1996, the sentinel still employs its original Fresnel lens.

Conzelman Road ends at the **Marin Headlands Visitor Center★**, which performs a dual function as a ranger station in a former military-post chapel. Hands-on exhibits introduce the natural and human history of the Headlands. Continue west around a picturesque lagoon to treacherous **Rodeo Beach**; its currents make it unsafe for swimming. The barracks of **Fort Cronkhite**, which once housed a Nike missile silo, overlook the beach.

Nearby is the **Marine Mammal Center**, an animal hospital that has rescued, rehabilitated and released hundreds of injured and sick marine mammals found on the California coast. Visitors can see adult and juvenile sea lions, seals and otters in various stages of recuperation.

Return to northbound US-101 and take the Shoreline Highway (Rte 1) west at the Mill Valley/Stinson Beach exit to reach kingly **Mt Tamalpais** (pronounced *tam-ul-PIE-us*). Named by its original Coast Miwok inhabitants – *tamal* means bay and *pa* means mountain – this rocky 2 571ft (793m) summit towers above San Francisco's northern horizon.

Turn right onto Panoramic Highway and follow signs to **Mt Tamalpais State Park★★**,

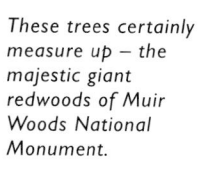

These trees certainly measure up – the majestic giant redwoods of Muir Woods National Monument.

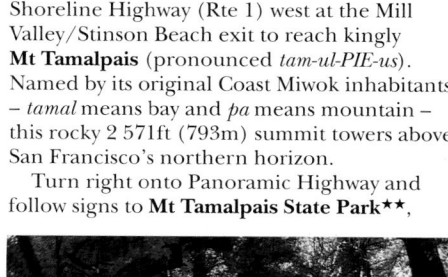

which cloaks the peak's western flanks. The
720-acre (291ha) park contains 210 miles
(326km) of hiking, biking and equestrian trails.

Those driving to the mountaintop will pass
numerous turnouts (lay-bys), picnic spots and
scenic vistas. From the summit, cities, towns
and bay appear as if on a giant raised relief
map, backdropped by Mt Diablo looming
35 miles (56km) to the east; it is one of the
finest panoramic **views★★★** in the Bay Area. On
clear winter days, the snow-capped Sierra
Nevada are visible 140 miles (224km) to the
east.

A nature lover's paradise, Mt Tamalpais is
blessed with abundant wildlife (including 300
species of birds) and a great variety of
vegetation. On the mountain's west slope,
along Redwood Creek completely surrounded
by the state park, **Muir Woods National
Monument★★★** has the largest stand of ancient
coast redwoods in the Bay Area. The grove of
majestic trees, some of them 250ft (77m) high,
attracts more than 2 million visitors annually.

You are advised to wear sturdy walking shoes
to explore Muir Woods. From the visitor center,
6 miles (9.6km) of mostly paved trails wind
though the forest and along Redwood and
Fern creeks. The 1 mile (1.6km) long Main
Trail crosses a series of wooden bridges and
loops under a dense canopy of mature
redwoods, the most impressive of which are in
the Cathedral and Bohemian groves. Trunks of
fallen giants in various states of decay nurture a
lush undergrowth of sword ferns, azaleas and
horsetail.

Further up the Marin coast, 40 miles (64km)
north of San Francisco beyond the charming
seaside communities of Stinson Beach and
Bolinas, is **Point Reyes National Seashore★★**.
The peninsula is windy, wave-swept and often
cloaked in fog, but its 102sq miles (264km²)

*No written
description can
prepare you for the
awesome majesty of
the giant redwoods,
some of them
already old before
Columbus set
sail!*

have long sandy beaches, lush forests, rugged sea cliffs and vast wetlands, all populated by a diverse animal, bird and marine life.

Exploration begins from the **Bear Valley Visitor Center★**. In addition to the fine natural history exhibits within the barnlike building, this is the starting point for short hikes along the 0.6 mile (1km) Earthquake Trail, which takes in the epicenter of the great tremor of 1906, and to the 100-acre (40ha) **Morgan Horse Farm**, whose muscular steeds are used by rangers for backcountry patrol.

Park maps will direct you 22 miles (35km) along Sir Francis Drake Blvd – past beaches, viewpoints, even an oyster farm – to the **Point Reyes Lighthouse★★**. Perched halfway down a sheer cliff, this beacon guided countless mariners along the rocky Pacific shore for a century after it began operating in 1870. A steep staircase of 308 steps, closed during high

Drakes Beach, one of the long, sandy stretches along Point Reyes National Seashore.

winds, descends to the station, where visitors can admire the three-ton Fresnel lens cast in 1867. The brass-mounted light is visible for more than 24 miles (40km) and is still fully operational. The spot is exceptionally popular with birdwatchers, who have recorded more than 360 species in the area, and with whale-watchers, who congregate to spot grey whales during their December-to-April migration season.

Pick another day to visit the bayside community of **Sausalito**★, nestled into the Marin Headlands a few miles north of the Golden Gate Bridge. Sausalito's sophisticated boutiques, winding streets and lush hillsides, dotted with attractive homes and gardens, create a relaxed ambience, and its privileged setting affords fine views of San Francisco and the bay islands.

The houseboat marina, Sausalito, offers alternative accommodation in this attractive settlement.

Enjoying a gourmet lunch at the Robert Mondavi Winery, Napa Valley.

Wine Country

Lying inland within a two-hour drive of San Francisco, the Napa Valley and Sonoma County thrive on the abundant sunshine and fertile soil that produce grapes for some of North America's finest wines. Though vineyards flourish along many of California's inland coastal areas from Eureka to San Diego County, and even as far east as the foothills of the Sierra Nevada, these areas just north of San Francisco are regarded as the pre-eminent US winemaking regions.

Northern California's first grapes, from Tokay cuttings, were planted in 1857 on a 400-acre (161ha) Sonoma estate by Hungarian immigrant Agoston Haraszthy. Today the Wine Country has moved beyond its traditional role to become a center for fine art and gastronomy. Trendy restaurants evince a growing dedication to the joys of pairing food and wine, and a new generation of showplace wineries combine wine production with innovative architecture.

The **Napa Valley★★**, cradled between two elongated mountain ranges, extends roughly 35 miles (56km) from San Pablo Bay north-west to Mt St Helena. Many of its best wineries

are clustered thickly along Hwy 29 as it passes
through the towns of Napa, Yountville,
Oakville, Rutherford, St Helena and Calistoga.
Others dot the tranquil Silverado Trail to the
east and the intervening crossroads.

Some of Napa's most interesting wineries,
from south to north include:

Codorniu Napa★ (1345 Henry Rd, off Old
Sonoma Rd, Napa) is a modern (1991) hillside
producer of Spanish-style sparkling wines.

Hess Collection Winery★★ (4411 Redwood Rd,
Napa) was built in 1903 and renovated in 1983.
It includes one of the largest private collections
of contemporary art in the US.

Domaine Chandon★ (1 California Dr, off Hwy
29, Yountville) is the perfect place to learn
about the tradition of French champagne.

Opus One★ (7900 Hwy 29, Oakville) is an ultra-
premium winery whose innovative 1991
architecture reflects a collaboration between
the French Baron de Rothschild and Napa
vintner Robert Mondavi (book tours in advance).

Robert Mondavi Winery★ (7801 Hwy 29,
Oakville) was the first of a new generation of
modern wineries (1966) showcasing local art
and architecture as well as wine.

St Supéry★★ (8440 Hwy 29, Rutherford)
incorporates a Wine Discovery Center with in-
depth displays and a 'smell-a-vision' exhibit.

Niebaum-Coppola★★ (1991 Hwy 29,
Rutherford), owned since 1975 by movie
maker Francis Ford Coppola, is an 1882 stone
winery with sets from his film, *The Godfather*.

Beringer Vineyards★★ (2000 Main St, St
Helena), Napa's oldest continuously operating
winery, was established in 1876 by the German
brothers. In the hillside behind are 1000ft
(300m) of tunnels for aging the wines.

Sterling Vineyards★★ (1111 Dunaweal Ln, off
Hwy 29, Calistoga) is perched like a Greek
monastery on a steep knoll that rises abruptly

from the valley, reached by an aerial tramway. **Clos Pegase★** (1060 Dunaweal Ln, off Hwy 29, Calistoga) was conceived by architect Michael Graves as a temple to wine and art.

Concurrent with winery visits – it's wise not to select more than four per day for tasting, and to limit guided tours to one or two per day – you may want to squeeze in another Napa sight or two.

The **Silverado Museum★**, in St Helena, is devoted to the life and works of 19C author Robert Louis Stevenson, who honeymooned in a cabin on the slopes of Mt St Helena in 1880 (a site now preserved in **Robert Louis Stevenson State Park**, 7 miles (11km) north of Calistoga on Hwy 29).

The **Culinary Institute of America at Greystone★** (Hwy 29, St Helena) is the West Coast campus of the most esteemed US school for food-and-wine professionals. Public tours enable you to watch chefs-to-be in action. There is a fine store (with wonderful cookbooks) and a collection of more than 1 800 corkscrews.

Vineyards near Calistoga, Napa Valley.

The little town of **Calistoga★**, at the head of the valley, is surrounded by geysers and hot springs. Several spa resorts operate on the town's main street, and its local airport is a base for ballooning enthusiasts.

West of Napa is **Sonoma County★★**, as well known for its historic attractions as its wineries. It was in the town of **Sonoma★★**, born in 1823 with the founding of the San Francisco Solano Mission, that California's independence movement was launched with the 1846 Bear Flag Revolt. Hoisting a white flag emblazoned with a brown bear and a star, a group of American settlers – disgruntled with Mexican control (and neglect) of California – proclaimed an independent republic. A month later, US forces captured Monterey, declared California a US possession, and effectively ended the short-lived republic.

Sonoma flourished as a supply and trade center in ensuing years. Today it retains the charm of the late 19C, especially in the historic adobe buildings facing its eight-acre central **Plaza★**. The City Hall (1908) stands at the heart of the park block, a dramatic bronze statue

The attractive central plaza of Sonoma has at its center the Mission Revival-style City Hall.

commemorating the Bear Flag Revolt.

The 19C buildings facing the Plaza on the north comprise the main part of **Sonoma State Historic Park★★**, which recalls the turbulence of the 1820s to 1850s. Start at **San Francisco Solano Mission★**, which served its parish for only 11 years before it was secularized in 1834. The original chapel exhibits authentic period paintings depicting the stations of the cross.

Across 1st St are the 1841 **Sonoma Barracks★**, a two-floor adobe that lodged Mexican and, later, US troops. Sleeping quarters have been re-created as part of its museum of Sonoma history. Next door, the **Toscano Hotel** was a general store when built in the 1850s, an immigrant boardinghouse in the 1880s.

The leading personality of 19C Sonoma was General Mariano Vallejo (1807-1890). His home, **Lachryma Montis★** ('tears of the mountain'), set beneath a hillside spring 1 mile (1.6km) north-west of the Plaza, is another part of the historic park. Built in Carpenter Gothic style amid expansive landscaped grounds, the fully furnished manor is a window into the past.

Before he built Lachryma Montis in 1850, Vallejo had a 100sq miles (259km²) livestock ranch at Petaluma, 10 miles (16km) west. A restoration of that ranch, **Petaluma Adobe★★**, comprises the final parcel of Sonoma State Historic Park. Authentic period pieces furnish many of its rooms and working areas.

East of the Plaza in Sonoma, **Sebastiani Vineyards★** (4th St East at E Spain St) boasts two 60 000-gallon (227 000-litre) oak fermentation tanks, among the world's largest. Haraszthy's original **Buena Vista Winery★★** (18000 Old Winery Rd, off Lovall Valley Rd) has the state's oldest winery building, the 1862 Press House, and extensive wine cellars dug into a limestone hill.

Literary enthusiasts won't want to miss **Jack London State Historic Park★★** near Glen Ellen, 10 miles (16km) north of Sonoma via Hwy 12 and London Ranch Rd. The San Francisco-born, Oakland-raised adventure writer (1876-1916) lived in these hills on a ranch during the last 11 years of his life. The park contains a fine exhibit of artifacts and manuscripts from his life and travels, and the ruins of Wolf House – a huge mansion he was building but which burned to the ground before he and his wife could move in.

East Bay

Two important cities on the east side of San Francisco Bay are connected to the peninsula by the Bay Bridge. **Oakland★**, with its bustling waterfront, has a fine historic district and an exceptional museum. **Berkeley★★** is best-known for its vibrant University of California campus, always at the cutting edge of academic innovation and cultural experimentation.

The modern Port of Oakland ranks among the 20 busiest in the world, with 11 marine terminals and 28 shipping berths that stretch

The bustling activity continues on the University of California campus, Berkeley.

for 19 miles (31km) along the bay and Oakland Estuary. A seven-block stretch of the once-gritty dock area now comprises **Jack London Square★**, an attractive complex of shops, restaurants, hotels, cinemas, nightclubs, a farmers' market and even a yacht harbor.

Oakland's rejuvenated downtown revolves around the fountained plazas of its high-rise **City Center★**. Opposite, on 14th St, rises **City Hall**, an imposing granite 1914 Beaux Arts structure with a Baroque-style clock tower. A 75ft (23m) glass rotunda links the twin towers of the monumental 1993 **Federal Building★**. The restored **Paramount Theatre★★**, 0.5 miles (0.8km) north of downtown on Broadway, is an outstanding example of Art Deco design in the spirit of great American movie palaces.

Near the southern shore of Lake Merritt, a large man-made saltwater lake surrounded by parkland, is the **Oakland Museum of California★★**. This masterful cultural complex, which opened in 1969, consolidated three previous museums devoted respectively to Native American ethnology and pioneer history, natural history and art. Designed by architect Kevin Roche, a colleague of the late Eero Saarinen, the museum features a series of tiered horizontal galleries overhung with roof gardens and fronting a central courtyard.

Each level interprets a different subject. On the first level, the **Hall of California Ecology** presents the state's geology, flora and fauna in dioramas that depict eight distinct biotic zones stretching east from coastline through High Sierra to desert. The **Cowell Hall of California History**, on the second level, traces human history through historical tableaux and displays of some 6 000 artifacts. The **Gallery of California Art**, on the third level, limited its collection to works (in all media) by artists who have lived, worked or studied in California.

WEATHER

San Francisco has a remarkably moderate climate of mild, wet winters and cool, dry summers. Geographically isolated, the city is shielded from continental temperature extremes by its coastal mountain ranges and the high Sierra Nevada to the east. Breezes off the Pacific Ocean, to the west, further temper spring and summer heat.

January is the coldest month, with average highs of 56°F (13°C) and average lows of 46°F (8°C). This is not dramatically different to September, the warmest month, with highs of 69°F (21°C) and lows of 56°F (13°C).

The city's annual 20in (50cm) of rainfall is not as evenly distributed, however. Far more rain falls in winter, with January having an average total of 4.6in (11.7cm), while during the five months of May to Sept combined only 0.86in (21.8mm) falls.

Summer is the windiest season, and for good reason. A fog bank sits on the cold coastal currents west of the city. In mid-summer, when temperatures in the state's Central Valley, 80 miles (128km) east, soar above 100°F (38°C) and stay there, the fog is drawn vacuum-like towards the heat (air always travels from cooler to warmer surfaces). Because the Golden Gate offers the only gap in hundreds of miles of mountainous shore, the fog thrusts through the mouth of San Francisco Bay. With the fog come the strong westerly winds which, in turn, dissipate the mist as they cool the land. Autumn days are relatively fog-free, and on these clear days the views are quite spectacular.

It is not easy to characterize the fickle weather patterns of this promontory. San Francisco's 43 hills foster peculiar microclimates. You're more likely to find sun and warmth, for instance, in the sheltered districts south of Market St (SoMa, the Mission, the Castro, etc), while Richmond, the Sunset and much of Golden Gate Park are shivering through a damp and cloudy day. On the other hand, the conditions may swap places in two hours. The bottom line is this: if you don't like the weather, wait a bit. By the time you finish your cup of espresso, it may well have cleared up.

GETTING AROUND

Despite its formidable hills, San Francisco is a wonderful city for walking. As one mid-1970s travel guide said, 'When you get tired of walking around San Francisco, you can always lean against it.'

Most visitor attractions are contained within a finite area of about 4 sq miles (10km²); those somewhat further away are easily reached by public transport or taxi. But walking remains the best way to capture the cosmopolitan spirit of this city and to turn up some serendipitous surprises as well.

Not that public transport is anything but excellent. The San Francisco Municipal Railway (Muni) operates an extensive network of diesel-powered buses, electric streetcars and cable cars throughout the city. The Bay Area Rapid Transit (BART) runs beneath the bay to link San Francisco with Oakland, Berkeley and other East Bay cities; an extension to the international airport is under construction. There's also a network of private ferry services, as befits a maritime city.

Fares are $1 for buses and streetcars, $2 for cable cars, slightly more for BART trains (with fares rated between destinations). If you plan extensive use of the Muni system within San Francisco, it is wise to purchase a Muni Passport. These allow unlimited travel on all systems (except BART) for one full day ($6), three days ($10) or seven days ($15), and also entitle holders to discounts at various Bay Area attractions.

Passports may be purchased, and system maps acquired, at the San Francisco Visitor Information Center (lower level, Hallidie Plaza, Market and Powell Sts), Tix Bay Area (Stockton St on Union Sq), or the Muni main office (949 Presidio Ave, Rm 238).

The landmark Ferry Building – once the hub of city transportation.

CALENDAR OF EVENTS

Consult the San Francisco Convention & Visitors Bureau or any of the numerous visitor publications for more information on these and other events.

Early February The colorful Chinese New Year Parade is the year's biggest event in North America's biggest Chinatown; tied in are a beauty pageant, flower market, street fair and other activities.

3rd Sunday in March The St Patrick's Day Parade, from Civic Center to the Embarcadero, brings out the green in everyone. It's followed by a night-long pub crawl.

Mid to late April The Cherry Blossom Festival at Japan Center is highlighted by Japanese music and dance, food booths and martial-arts displays.

3rd Sunday in May The Bay to Breakers Foot Race, sponsored by the *Examiner* newspaper, inspires 80 000 runners, many in zany costumes, to run 7 miles (11km) from the Embarcadero to Ocean Beach.

Memorial Day weekend More than half a million spectators attend Carnaval, which dominates Mission and Harrison Sts in the Mission District. Salsa music and samba dancing are part of the huge parade.

Mid-June weekend The North Beach Festival (Grant Ave between Vallejo and Union Sts) is said to be the oldest urban street

Chinese New Year Parade.

fair in the US. There are food and crafts booths, live entertainment and more.

Last Sunday in June As many as half a million people march in the Lesbian, Gay, Bisexual, Transgender Pride Celebration down Market St from the Castro District to the Embarcadero.

3rd Thursday in July It's safe to say the Cable Car Bell-Ringing Championship at Union Square is a singular event. Gripmen compete by clanging out melodies on the vehicles' bells as they roll down Powell St.

Labor Day weekend This is San Francisco's annual 'food-sampling' festival. Get into the flavor of the 50 restaurants, 20 microbreweries and 20 wineries who offer fare in Golden Gate Park.

Labor Day weekend At the Sausalito Art Festival in Marinship Park, 11 000 original artworks from around the world are shown, and there's plenty of food and music.

Mid-September weekend San Francisco's seafaring past is re-created during the Festival of the Sea at Hyde St Pier. Included are a parade of historic ships, sea shanties, dancing and boat rides.

1st or 2nd Sunday in October Italian Heritage Parade in North Beach is highlighted by a march from Fisherman's Wharf to celebrate the landing of Christopher Columbus in America.

31 October Halloween is a huge holiday, thanks in large part to the gay community. You'll see the most imaginative costumes in the Castro. Inquire about the Exotic Erotic Halloween Ball, held the previous weekend.

ACCOMMODATIONS

San Francisco offers a full spectrum of possibilities, from world-class hotels to youth hostels. In between is a wide range of options: moderately priced hotels and B&Bs (bed-and-breakfast homes), lower priced motels, apartments and student dormitories (available seasonally). It's even possible to find 'boat-and-breakfast'.

Generally speaking, San Francisco is an expensive city to visit, particularly if you intend to stay midtown. (Less costly lodgings are typically a bus or train ride away.) For a double room at a luxury hotel, you should expect to pay at least $200 per night, sometimes even $300. Mid-priced hotels will run upwards of $150, while moderate hotels charge $100 and over. Most B&Bs are in the moderate range as well. Should a midtown hotel offer you a rate considerably less than $100 per night, you'd be wise to inspect the room (and environs) before accepting. Prices for single occupants are often the same, and rarely significantly less, than the double rate. Bear in mind that quoted prices don't include an additional 14% in hotel tax. Except in B&Bs, breakfast is not normally included in the rate, either.

Many San Francisco visitors prefer to stay in smaller 'boutique' hotels, moderately to mid-priced, feeling they reflect the historic character of the city in ways that large, modern national hotel chains cannot. Many of these small luxury hotels are owned by one of two groups that can assist in pairing properties with personalities. Contact: the **Kimpton Group**, 222 Kearny St, Suite 200, SF 94108 ☎ **415 397 5572**; and **Joie de Vivre Hotels**, 567 Sutter St, SF 94102 ☎ **415 835 0300**.

Leading national chains with locations in the San Francisco Bay Area include:
Best Western ☎ **800 528 1234**
Comfort Inn ☎ **800 228 5150**
Hilton ☎ **800 445 8667**
Holiday Inn ☎ **800 465 4329**
Hyatt ☎ **800 233 1234**
ITT Sheraton ☎ **800 325 3535**
Marriott ☎ **800 228 9290**
Ramada ☎ **800 228 2828**
Ritz-Carlton ☎ **800 241 3333**
Westin ☎ **800 228 3000**

If you need help finding a room, contact one of the following toll-free (freephone) reservation-service numbers:
Accommodations Express ☎ **800 444 7666**
California Reservations ☎ **800 576 0003**

Central Reservation Services ☎ **800 548 3311**
Hotel Reservation Network ☎ **800 964 6835**
San Francisco Reservations ☎ **800 737 2060**
SF Trips ☎ **800 738 7477**

Contact **Bed & Breakfast San Francisco** ☎ **415 479 1913** or **800 452 8249** for a B&B placement. (*Note that these 800 toll-free/free-phone numbers may not be accessible outside the US.*)

For those on a tight budget, Hostelling International operates two facilities in the city: the **Union Square Youth Hostel**, downtown at 312 Mason St, SF 94102, ☎ **415 788 5604**; and the **Fort Mason Youth Hostel**, in the Marina District at Building 240, Fort Mason, SF 94123, ☎ **415 771 7277**. These include dormitory-style lodging and shared kitchen and bathroom facilities. YHA membership is required but can be obtained on the spot. **European Guest House**, a member of the American Association of International Hostels, also offers accommodations in the city at 761 Minna St, SF 94103, ☎ **415 861 6634**.

Furnished apartment rentals – which start at around $100 a day, making them ideal for groups traveling together – are available through **American Property Exchange**, 2800 Van Ness Ave, SF 94109, ☎ **415 447 2040** or **800 747 7784**.

Recommendations
Over $200

Campton Place Hotel (340 Stockton St, SF 94108, ☎ **415 781 5555**) Mid-size luxury hotel with superb service at Union Square.

Fairmont Hotel & Tower (950 Mason St, SF 94108, ☎ **415 772 5000**) Grand historic hotel on Nob Hill.

$150-$200

Hyatt Regency San Francisco (5 Embarcadero Center, SF 94111, ☎ **415 788 1234**) Spectacular hotel with 17-floor central atrium at foot of Market St.

Hotel Monaco (501 Geary St, SF 94102, ☎ **415 292 0100**) Theater District boutique hotel, a remodeled 1910 Beaux Arts classic.

Prescott Hotel (545 Post St, SF 94102, ☎ **415 563 0303**) Boutique hotel with great rooms and service just off Union Square.

$100-$150

Chancellor Hotel (433 Powell St, SF 94102, ☎ **415 362 2004**) A stately and dependable standby on the cable car line, half a block from Union Square.

Phoenix Hotel (601 Eddy St, SF 94109, ☎ **415 776 1380**) Hippest hotel in town and a rockers' paradise with its swimming pool fringed by palm trees.

Hotel Triton (342 Grant Ave, SF 94108, ☎ **415 394 0500**) Colorful avant-garde boutique hotel at Chinatown Gate.

$50-$100

Andrews Hotel (624 Post St, SF 94109, ☎ **415 563 6877**) Pleasant, classic Victorian hotel near Union Square.

Grant Plaza (465 Grant Ave, SF 94108, ☎ **415 434 3883**) Clean and bright bargain in Chinatown; good value.

24 Henry Guesthouse (24 Henry St, SF 94114, ☎ **415 864 5686**) Gay-oriented B&B in one of the Castro District's fine 19C Victorian homes.

Attractive bed-and-breakfast hotels can be found on Union Street, Cow Hollow.

FOOD AND DRINK

San Franciscans are curious and demanding diners. Their willingness to experiment with new cuisines and with innovative interpretations of traditional dishes has earned the city a well-deserved reputation for fine dining. This devotion to the eating experience, fueled and sated by a dedicated legion of celebrity chefs, has elevated dining in the area to the level of high art. The seafood in particular is outstanding, complemented by the fine wines of the nearby Napa and Sonoma regions.

The region's multi-ethnic heritage also has created a restaurant environment in which international specialties happily coexist. Especially prevalent is Asian cooking, and not just authentic Chinese and Japanese, Thai and Indian cuisines. Here you'll find restaurants that offer

Stained glass window, Niebaum-Coppola Winery, Napa Valley.

Afghani, Burmese, Cambodian, Indonesian, Korean, Tibetan and others rarely found in the US. A trend among inventive chefs is 'Asian fusion', which takes the best elements of various national dishes and blends them with regional ingredients to intrigue the palate.

There's no one place to find great food in this city. A neighborhood with an ethnic orientation, naturally, is the best place to find restaurants of that ilk: Chinatown (and the Richmond District) for Chinese, North Beach for Italian, the Mission for Mexican and other Latin cuisines. Visit Fisherman's Wharf for seafood. Union Square, Civic Center and the Financial District are strong in American and Continental cuisines; the rekindled SoMa and Embarcadero areas are the current hot spots for innovative new American restaurants. Neighborhoods like the Marina, Cow Hollow and Richmond all have a fine variety of creative and ethnic eateries.

Recommendations

Prices in the following listing indicate the average cost of an entree, an appetizer or dessert, and a drink.

Over $50

Chez Panisse (1517 Shattuck Ave, Berkeley) Craftsman-style restaurant that begat the California cuisine craze in the 1970s.

The French Laundry (6640 Washington St, Yountville) Lavish and creative prix-fixe restaurant in the Wine Country.

Jardiniere (300 Grove St, Civic Center) Wildly innovative continental dishes in a 2-story theater of spectacular design.

Masa's (648 Bush St, Union Sq) Superb prix-fixe French dinners in a luxurious and intimate setting.

$30-$50

Alioto's (8 Fisherman's Wharf) Sicilian seafood restaurant whose sidewalk frontage features the fastest crab-cracker on the bay.

Anjou (44 Campton Pl, Union Sq) Classic French restaurant with memorable foie gras, hidden in a small urban lane.

Fior d'Italia (601 Union St, North Beach) On Washington Park, claims to be America's oldest Italian restaurant: it opened in 1886.

Hawthorne Lane (22 Hawthorne Ln, SoMa) Bright and busy California-Asian restaurant on small alley behind MOMA.

McCormick & Kuleto's (Ghirardelli Sq, Fisherman's Wharf) Spacious restaurant with superb grilled seafood and fine views.

Moose's (1652 Stockton St, North Beach) Creative Mediterranean eatery that lures civic leaders to Washington Square.

Rose Pistola (532 Columbus Ave, North Beach) Lively Italian winner of the 1997 James Beard

Fisherman's Wharf sign.

award for best new restaurant in US.

Wine Spectator Greystone Restaurant (2555 Main St, St Helena) 'Educational' dining establishment in Wine Country, attached to Culinary Institute of America.

$15-$30

Betelnut Pejiu Wu (2030 Union St, Cow Hollow) Far Eastern 'street food' in a red-lacquered, bamboo-accented 'Asian beer house'.

Café de la Presse (352 Grant Ave, Union Sq) Casual French meals at an international news-stand beside Chinatown Gate.

Green's (Bldg A, Fort Mason Center, Marina District) Innovative vegetarian spot with great view of the Golden Gate Bridge.

Leon's BBQ (1911 Fillmore St, Pacific Hts) Long, narrow 'dive' in ritzy area; famous for its pork ribs.

Max's Opera Cafe (601 Van Ness Ave, Civic Center) Boasts a cast of singing waiters and waitresses.

Mustards Grill (7399 St Helena Hwy, Yountville) Casual and popular gathering place for winemakers and industry VIPs.

Scala's Bistro (432 Powell St, Union Sq) Attractive French-Italian bistro with arty decor, fine service and lively bar scene.

Tadich Grill (240 California St, Financial Dist) Gold Rush institution with long wooden bar and great grilled fish.

Under $15

Hamburger Mary's (1582 Folsom St, SoMa) Classic burger joint that attracts many of the tattooed and pierced set.

Lhasa Moon (2420 Lombard St, Cow Hollow) Tibetan immigrant-run restaurant that offers a true adventure in dining.

Mario's Bohemian Cigar Store Café (566 Columbus Ave, North Beach) Quaint corner café noted for toasted focaccia sandwiches.

Rassellas (2801 California St, Pacific Hts) Spicy Ethiopian food served in a dark, exotic atmosphere with nightly jazz.

Sears Fine Foods (Chancellor Hotel, 439 Powell St, Union Sq) Campy diner with frumpy waitresses and famous pancakes.

Ti Couz (3108 16th St, Mission District) Guarantees lines (queues) for its savory and sweet Breton crepes; busy wine bar.

SHOPPING

From large complexes that incorporate national chains with entertainment venues and restaurants, to intimate rows of boutiques scattered throughout the city, San Francisco will satisfy even the most ardent shopper.

Union Square, considered the city's main shopping district, is home to its major department stores. They include **Macy's** (Stockton and O'Farrell Sts), **Neiman Marcus** (150 Stockton St), **Gump's** (135 Post St) and **Saks Fifth Avenue** (384 Post St). Both **Emporium** and **Nordstrom** are located a few blocks away in the **San Francisco Centre** (865 Market St), a 9-floor complex of more than 100 shops and restaurants. Designer boutiques and specialty shops can be found on and near Post St, Sutter St and Maiden Lane.

San Francisco's largest concentration of art galleries is along Geary, Sutter, Post and Powell Sts. The *San Francisco Gallery Guide*, published bimonthly (and available free in most hotels and galleries), provides a comprehensive listing of current exhibits and their locations.

In the **Financial District** is the **Embarcadero Center**, a 10-acre office and retail complex incorporating more than 125 shops and restaurants. The **Crocker Galleria** (50 Post St) contains some 50 designer and specialty shops. More than 25 fine antique shops are located in the **Jackson Square Historic District** north of the TransAmerica Pyramid, near Jackson and Montgomery Sts.

In bustling **Chinatown**, you can haggle at an open-air market, admire luxurious silks and jades in fine shops, or purchase traditional Asian herbal remedies in pharmacies. You can also find a wide selection of shoddily produced souvenirs.

Four major retail centers punctuate **Fisherman's Wharf**'s festive strip of souvenir shops and novelty museums. **The Anchorage** has close to 50 shops and restaurants; **The Cannery** houses some 40 specialty shops and eating establishments; **Ghirardelli Square** features more than 70 shops, including major retail chains; and **Pier 39** boasts over 100 specialty and gift shops.

Most stores accept major credit cards and travelers' checks (travellers' cheques), but not out-of-state checks (cheques). The San Francisco Convention and Visitors Bureau can offer detailed information on types of shops, locations and opening hours.

Neighborhood shopping includes:

Castro District (Castro St between 16th & 19th Sts) Window-shopping and people-watching are primary pursuits in the city's main gay neighborhood.

Civic Center (Hayes St between Franklin & Buchanan Sts) Antiques, hip fashions and avant-garde art, a stone's throw from City Hall.

Cow Hollow (Union St between Van Ness Ave & Steiner St) Gentrified and often overpriced shopping strip with plenty of boutiques and galleries.

Haight-Ashbury (Haight St between Stanyan St & Fillmore St) Vintage clothing stores, art galleries, record shops and bookstores, many reflecting the erstwhile heartbeat of San Francisco counterculture.

Marina District (Chestnut St between Divisadero & Fillmore

Taking five in Ghirardelli Square.

Sts) Great shops for the younger postgraduate crowd.

Mission District (24th St between Mission St & Potrero Ave, and Valencia St between 16th & 23rd Sts) Markets and shops sell Latino imports, including arts and crafts, jewelry and clothing. Shops tend to be traditional along 24th, more avant-garde on Valencia.

Pacific Heights (Fillmore St between Jackson & Ellis Sts) High quality galleries and boutiques with fashion clothing at often-moderate prices.

South of Market (various locations) A bargain hunter's dream, this area – which should be explored by car rather than on foot – incorporates dozens of outlet centers, resale shops and design showrooms.

ENTERTAINMENT AND NIGHTLIFE

Many dozens of diversions take place nightly (and especially at weekends) throughout San Francisco and the greater Bay Area. From classic performing arts like symphony and opera; to stage productions that ranges from off-Broadway musicals to experimental attic productions; to nightclubs catering on one hand to elderly swing-music aficionados, on the other to gay and lesbian party-lovers. There is something to entertain everyone.

Performing Arts

Symphony, opera, theater, ballet, modern and international dance,

The Louise M Davies Symphony Hall.

and other 'high' arts performances may sell out months in advance, so it's wise to buy tickets early. Full-price tickets can be purchased directly from the venue's box office or from one of the brokers listed below. Major credit cards are accepted (a service charge of $1 to $7 typically is added to the ticket price). Ticket brokers sometimes have tickets available when the box office has sold out, but expect to pay a service charge up to as much as 25%. Hotel concierges also may be able to secure tickets at short notice.

Bass Ticketmaster (☎ 510 762 2277) seemingly has tickets for everything; outlets are at most locations of Tower Records (including 2525 Jones St, Fisherman's Wharf) and Sound Warehouse (including 30 Powell St, Union Sq). **Tix Bay Area** on Union Square (Stockton St between Post and Geary Sts, ☎ 415 433 7827) offers half-price tickets for selected events on the day of the show. **City Box Office** (152 Kearny St, ☎ 415 392 4400) specializes in classical performances at smaller venues.

The Bay Area's most important centers for the performing arts are these:

Cow Palace (2600 Geneva Ave, Daly City, ☎ 415 469 6065), just south of San Francisco, luring rock groups and other national touring companies.

Louise M Davies Symphony Hall (201 Van Ness Ave, Civic Center, ☎ 415 552 8000) Home of the San Francisco Symphony Orchestra.
Paramount Theatre (2025 Broadway, Oakland, ☎ 510 465 6400) Art-deco home of the Oakland Ballet and East Bay Symphony Orchestra.
War Memorial Opera House (301 Van Ness Ave, Civic Center, ☎ 415 864 3330) Home of the San Francisco Ballet and San Francisco Opera.
Yerba Buena Center for the Arts (700 Howard St, SoMa, ☎ 415 978 2787) Modern theater complex at Yerba Buena Gardens, home to the San Francisco Contemporary Music Players.
Zellerbach Hall (Bancroft Wy & Dana St, University of California, Berkeley, ☎ 510 642 9988) Where Cal Performances stages a rich and varied annual series of music and dance productions.

Theaters

Leading theaters include the following:
Berkeley Repertory Theater (2025 Addison St, Berkeley ☎ 510 845 4700) A leading regional theater company.
Cable Car Theater (430 Mason St, Theater Dist ☎ 415 956 8497) Offering an eclectic variety of plays, musicals and solo performances.
Club Fugazi (678 Green St, North Beach ☎ 415 421 4222) Home of

San Francisco's 23-year musical-comedy phenomenon, *Beach Blanket Babylon.*

Cowell Theater (Pier 2, Fort Mason Center ☎ 415 441 3687) Offers concerts and dance performances as well as musical and comedy productions.

Curran Theatre (445 Geary St, Theater Dist ☎ 415 474 3800) Prime showcase for touring Broadway productions like *Phantom of the Opera.*

EXIT Theater (156 Eddy St, Union Sq ☎ 415 751 0439) Producer of the SF Fringe Festival; offers experimental works in a bohemian cabaret atmosphere.

Geary Theater (415 Geary St, Theater Dist ☎ 415 749 2228) Home of San Francisco's premier acting troupe, the American Conservatory Theater Company.

Golden Gate Theater (1 Taylor St at Market St ☎ 415 474 3800) Major venue for mainstream shows.

Herbst Theatre (401 Van Ness Ave, Civic Center ☎ 415 392 4400) 1 000-seat theater in the Veterans Building, host to classical and contemporary productions.

Mason St Theatre (340 Mason St, Theater Dist ☎ 415 982 5463) A second-floor room that is home to the long-running comedy-mystery *Shear Madness.*

New Conservatory Theater (25 Van Ness Ave, Civic Center ☎ 415 861 8972) Stages new and traditional plays in an art-gallery setting.

Theatre on the Square (450 Post St, Union Sq ☎ 415 433 9500) Presents fine contemporary productions, from drama to musical comedy.

Live Music

For information on current happenings in the San Francisco area, check the 'Datebook' section of the Sunday *San Francisco Examiner and Chronicle,* or consult listings in either of two free alternative weeklies, the *San Francisco Weekly* and the *San Francisco Bay Guardian.*

Rock

The Fillmore Auditorium (1805 Geary Blvd, Japantown) Renovated 1960s auditorium, attracting important rock acts.

Great American Music Hall (859 O'Farrell St, Tenderloin) Traditional theater offering cabaret-style acts, often by touring big-name performers.

Slim's (333 11th St, SoMa) 300-seat club owned by singer Boz Scaggs, draws SRO crowds to see top touring and local rock, jazz and blues bands.

Blues

Biscuits & Blues (401 Mason St, Theater Dist) Spacious basement club with live show lineup including top names in blues.

Boom Boom Boom (1601 Fillmore St, Pacific Hts) Owned by John Lee Hooker, one of the genre's venerable geniuses, re-creates an old-time blues joint.

Jazz
Café du Nord (2170 Market St, near Castro) Hip basement speakeasy that features swing and salsa, jazz and cabaret.

Jazz at Pearl's (256 Columbus Ave, North Beach) Spacious long-time club featuring contemporary jazz combos.

Up & Down Club (1151 Folsom St, SoMa) Chic, elegant acid-jazz supper club downstairs, vinyl-boothed disco upstairs.

Yoshi's (Jack London Sq, Oakland), Japanese restaurant/jazz club that imports major touring acts for several nights at a time.

Swing
Coconut Grove (1415 Van Ness Ave, Polk Gulch) Sophisticated supper club with torch-song ambience and tropical decor.

Starlight Room (Sir Francis Drake Hotel, 450 Powell St, Union Sq) The 21st-floor lounge, with big-band music, has wonderful views.

Top of the Mark (Mark Hopkins Inter-Continental Hotel, 1 Nob Hill) World-famous 19th-floor hilltop lounge with big-band music for adults of all ages.

The Castro Theatre is the city's finest example of an early-20C movie-palace.

Salsa
Sol y Luna (475 Sacramento St, Financial Dist) Lively Latin supper club with Flamenco dancing, jazz and a late-night tapas menu.

Bars
Buena Vista (2765 Hyde St, Fisherman's Wharf) Old-time café known as the 'home of Irish coffee in America'.

Carnelian Room (Bank of American Bldg, 555 California St, Financial Dist) Heady view from 52nd floor (jackets and ties required).

Li Po Cocktail Lounge (916 Grant St, Chinatown) Local 'dive' straight from a Charlie Chan movie with a Buddhist shrine behind the bar and giant rice-paper lantern.

The Red Room (The Commodore, 827 Sutter St, Union Sq) Classy avant-garde lounge where everything is red, from floors to furniture and lighting.

Redwood Room (Clift Hotel, 495 Geary St, Union Sq) Piano and cigar bar built from the wood of a single redwood tree felled in 1934.

Spec's 12 Adler Museum Café (12 Saroyan Pl at 250 Columbus Ave, North Beach) Secluded alleyway bar worth visiting to see collection of Barbary Coast junk.

Twin Peaks Tavern (401 Castro St, Castro Dist) America's oldest gay bar, quiet but crowded room that draws a 40-plus clientele to the corner of Market St.

SPORTS

Spectator Sports
American Football is the hot ticket in the Bay Area, with two highly successful professional teams playing on opposite sides of the Bay. The San Francisco '49ers (☎ **415 656 4949**), a perennial Super Bowl contender (and frequent winner in the early 1990s), play their games at 3Com Park at Candlestick Point, while the Oakland Raiders (☎ **510 615 1888**) perform in the Oakland Coliseum. The 16-game National Football League season lasts from late August to December, with championship playoffs continuing into January.

The major-league **baseball** season begins at the end of March; teams play 162 games, continuing into October with World Series playoffs. Again, the Bay Area has two teams. The San Francisco Giants (☎ **415 467 8000**) of the National League are scheduled to move from 3Com Park to a new stadium at China Basin in 2000. The American League's Oakland A's (☎ **510 568 5600**) perform at Oakland Coliseum.

The Golden State Warriors (☎ **510 986 2200**) are the area's lone professional **basketball** representatives. The National Basketball Association team plays an 82-game season from November to April; subsequent playoffs can last into June. Home games are at Oakland Coliseum.

Participatory Sports

San Francisco's northern waterfront, from Fort Basin through the Presidio to Ocean Beach, provides excellent on-street **bicycling**. Off-road (mountain biking) enthusiasts look north to Marin and Mt Tamalpais.

There are numerous **golf** courses in the Bay Area; those in the city itself include the nine-hole, par-27 Golden Gate Park Course and formal 18-hole courses at Hardin Park (Lake Merced), Lincoln Park (Sutro Heights), and the Presidio.

Serious golfers set their sights south on the Pebble Beach courses on the Monterey Peninsula.

As might be expected of a maritime community, **water sports** are extremely popular. There are numerous sailing clubs, scuba diving shops, and rental locations for both windsurfing and sea-kayaking, with instruction available at all pursuits.

Mountain biking in the Golden Gate National Recreation Area.

THE BASICS

This guide is intended for overseas visitors as well as those from the US and Canada. Some details will not apply to everyone.

Before You Go

Citizens of the United Kingdom and the 20 other countries (including New Zealand) that participate in the Visa Waiver Pilot Program (VWPP), do not require a visitor's visa to enter the US as ordinary tourists for a period of up to 90 days. All that is needed are a valid passport, a round-trip transportation ticket and a visa waiver form, which may be obtained from a travel agent in advance, or from an airline during check-in. This form must be handed to immigration officials upon arrival. Visas are required for certain categories of visitor, including those planning to study or do business within the US.

Visitors from most other countries must carry a valid passport and a non-immigrant visitor's visa. Details are available from the nearest US embassy or consulate.

Vaccinations are not required.

Getting There
By Air

Direct flights arrive at San Francisco International Airport (SFO) (☎ 650 876 7809) from all over the world, particularly from the Asia-Pacific realm but also from London and Europe. There is a huge network of flight connections throughout North America.

Taxis, hotel shuttles and public buses wait outside the baggage claim area, and a Bay Area Rapid Transit (BART) rail link is under construction. The terminal is 13.5 miles (21.7km) south of downtown San Francisco, a drive of no more than 25 minutes except when rush-hour traffic is heavy.

Oakland International Airport (OAK) (☎ 510 577 4000) flights are limited to domestic connections. This airport, preferred by some commuters because it is small and easy to get around, is 7.5 miles (12km) south of downtown Oakland and 17 miles (27km) from central San Francisco.

By Rail

Amtrak (☎ 800 872 7245) service to the Bay Area ends at Emeryville, adjacent to Berkeley. From there, a free shuttle bus takes passengers across the Bay Bridge to San Francisco's Ferry Building, on the Embarcadero. The major long-distance route to the Bay Area is from Chicago (via Denver and Salt Lake; 49hrs). A route from Los Angeles (11hrs) ends in Oakland, with shuttle transport to San Francisco's Transbay Terminal.

By Car

San Francisco is easily reached by major national highways. Interstate 80 crosses the Bay Bridge from the east; Interstate 280 enters the city from the south; US 101 crosses the Golden Gate Bridge from the north. Parking can be a problem in the downtown area, although most hotels have arrangements with (often expensive) parking garages. *See also* **Car Rental** and **Driving**

By Bus

Greyhound Lines (☎ **800 231 2222** or **415 495 6789**) provide leisurely access to the Bay Area from all corners of North America, at a cost generally lower than other forms of public transportation. Buses arrive at San Francisco's Transbay Terminal (First and Mission Sts, SoMa).

Fisherman's Wharf, with Telegraph Hill in the distance.

A-Z

Accidents and Breakdowns

If you're driving a rented vehicle, check to see if your rental agreement includes collision damage waiver (CDW), a form of insurance that covers the car you are driving. It is not cheap (between $9 and $13 a day), but without it you are liable for every scratch and bump on the car. If it does not come with the deal, it is well worth adding it on, unless your own policy covers you.

An emergency telephone number will be provided for your use in case your car breaks down. A mobile phone, which may be rented from the agency, will offer a lifeline in an emergency. Women driving alone are advised not to advertise the fact that they are in trouble.

Following any accident or breakdown, pull your car over to the side of the road and raise your car hood (bonnet), ☎ 911 for police, ambulance or fire, and wait for the highway patrol or other emergency services to arrive. If you belong to the American Automobile Associa-tion or associated overseas motorists' club, ☎ 800 222 4357 for emergency road assistance.

Accommodations see p.97

Airports

see **Getting There, p.110**

Alcoholic Beverages

The legal minimum age for purchase and consumption of alcoholic beverages is 21. Proof of age is required. Legal hours of sale are 6am-2am, and most bars stay open until 2am. Almost all packaged-goods stores sell beer, wine and liquor (spirits).

Banks

These are open weekdays, usually Mon-Thur, 9am-4pm, and 9am-5pm or 6pm Friday. Some banks also open on Saturdays from 9am-1pm.

Most banks change travelers' checks (cheques) and currency for a small commission. You may get slightly better rates at exchange service agencies. It is wise to bring checks (cheques) in US dollar amounts, as these are widely accepted as cash.

Visitors from around the world have access to cash withdrawals, using major credit cards and bank cards, at the 24-hour automatic teller machines (ATMs) outside most banks. You can get lists of outlets and charges from your home bank before departing on your trip. *See also* **Money**

Beaches

Despite its maritime location, San Francisco is not regarded as a beach city. Cold offshore currents and prevailing winds leave the shoreline uninviting most of the year. Hardy souls not intimidated by dangerous undertows and stiff breezes head to Ocean Beach 3 miles (5km) away and – north of that, around the flank of Sutro Heights and the Presidio – little Land's End, China and Baker beaches. Tiny Aquatic Park Beach, wedged between Fisherman's Wharf and Fort Mason, is the only such strand on San Francisco Bay.

Marin County's best watersports destination is Stinson Beach, 22 miles (35km) north of San Francisco on Hwy 1, while Pescadero State Beach, 38 miles (61km) south of the city, draws beachgoers to the Peninsula. The most popular beach in the greater Bay Area, however, is Santa Cruz, 82 miles (132km) south. Its restored boardwalk preserves the appeal of an old seaside amusement park.

Bicycles

Because of its steep hills, San Francisco is not often regarded as an ideal place for cycling. Exceptions are the bayshore, particularly from the Marina District east past Fisherman's Wharf to the Embarcadero, and west through the Presidio to Ocean Beach. Many streets have designated bike lanes, and you'll find rentals in various locations including Golden Gate Park. Mountain biking is especially popular in the hills of Marin County and East Bay.

Books

With its long and fascinating literary history, San Francisco has a surfeit of books in which the city plays as big a role as its characters. Here are a few suggestions:

Herb Caen, *The Best of Herb Caen*
Tom Cole, *A Short History of San Francisco*
Allen Ginsberg, *Howl and Other Poems*
Herbert Gold, *Travels in San Francisco*
Dashiell Hammett, *The Maltese Falcon*
John Jakes, *California Gold*
Jack Kerouac, *The Subterraneans*
Jack London, *Martin Eden*
Armistead Maupin, *Tales of the City*

Frank Norris, *McTeague*
Robert Louis Stevenson, *The Silverado Squatters*
Amy Tan, *The Joy Luck Club*
Mark Twain, *Roughing It*
Tom Wolfe, *The Electric Kool-Aid Acid Test*

Buses
see **Getting Around, p.95**

Camping
While there's nowhere in San Francisco itself to pitch a tent, there are numerous places in the hinterlands. Nearest are Mt Tamalpais State Park and Point Reyes National Recreation Area, north of the city; Portola, Butano, Castle Rock and other state parks south of Palo Alto, on the lower Peninsula; Mt Diablo State Park, over the East Bay hills from Oakland. Get details from the California Dept of Parks & Recreation or the National Park Service.

Car Rental
Unless you're planning an excursion outside San Francisco – to Marin County or the Wine Country, for example – it probably doesn't make sense to rent a vehicle during your stay. You can explore the city easily on foot or using public transport.

If you do decide to rent a car, you'll find them widely available at the airport and through hotels and individual agencies. Prices may vary a great deal, so compare prices before you book. Generally they are lower in the US than in other countries. Considerable discounts may be available if you reserve well in advance.

The minimum rental age is 21, although some companies impose a limit of 25, and others increase insurance premiums for those under 25. You must have a valid driver's license. You will be expected to pay by credit card, and if you don't have one, you may be required to pay a large deposit.

Rental cars in the US are usually equipped with automatic transmission. Try to get free unlimited mileage; note that there will probably be a drop-off charge if you leave the car at a different location. You may wish to buy a collision damage waiver (CDW) when you rent the vehicle. *See* **Accidents and Breakdowns** for details on this; *also see* **Driving**

Children
Most visitor attractions in San Francisco offer reduced admission to those under 18 years of age. The lion's share of these sights are either in the Fisherman's Wharf area (including bay cruises, historic ships and amusements) or at Golden Gate Park (California Academy of Sciences, various recreational activities).

Other attractions of special interest to the younger set include the Exploratorium interactive science museum and the San Francisco Zoo.

Many hotels allow children under 18 to stay in their parents' rooms free of charge, while others may offer family discount rates. Some larger properties may provide day care, evening babysitting, or organized activities for children. Restaurants, particularly national chains, often have special menus, small portions and games.

San Francisco has its own children's theater and fine-arts groups, and in summer the public library hosts numerous special children's events. Ask at the Tourist Information Offices for monthly events calendars.

Churches see Religion

Climate see p.94

Clothing

As a general rule, you can plan to dress in casual, comfortable clothes during your visit to San Francisco. Some leading hotels and restaurants require that men wear jackets and ties, and if you're planning an evening at the opera, ballet, symphony (concert) or major theater, formal dress is appropriate.

The volatile nature of the city's weather means it is advisable always to have a warm sweater and raincoat or umbrella handy. As summers here are cooler than in any other major US city, you probably won't often need shorts or T-shirts. Jeans and button-down shirts are more suitable.

Measurements in the US are still imperial. Clothing sizes are always two figures less than they are in the UK, with the exception of men's suits and shirts (which are identical). UK shoe sizes and women's clothes sizes differ from the US as follows:

Dress Sizes

US	6	8	10	12	14	16
UK	8	10	12	14	16	18

Women's Shoes

US	6	6.5	7	7.5	8	8.5
UK	4.5	5	5.5	6	6.5	7

Men's Shoes

US	8	8.5	9.5	10.5	11.5	12
UK	7	7.5	8.5	9.5	10.5	11

Pebble Beach Golf Course.

Complaints

Make any complaints at a hotel, restaurant or store to the manager. For more serious complaints, report the problem to a Tourist Information Office or, as in the case of theft, contact the police ☎ 911.

Consulates

The nearest consulates for English-speaking countries are at the following addresses:

British Consulate
1 Sansome St, Suite 850
San Francisco, CA 94104
☎ 415 981 3030

Australian Consulate
1 Bush St, Suite 700
San Francisco, CA 94104
☎ 415 362 6160

Canadian Consulate
300 S Grand Ave, Suite 1000
Los Angeles, CA 90071
☎ 213 346 2700

Irish Consulate
44 Montgomery St, Suite 3830
San Francisco, CA 94104
☎ 415 392 4214

New Zealand Consulate
1 Maritime Plaza, Suite 700
San Francisco, CA 94111
☎ 415 399 1255

Crime

San Francisco is considered a relatively safe city, but muggings and theft do occur. These common-sense precautions are recommended to ensure a safe and enjoyable visit:

- Avoid carrying large sums of money, and don't let others see how much you are carrying. Keep additional cash and credit cards in your hotel safe.
- Keep a firm hold of purses and knapsacks, carry your wallet in a secure (front) pocket, and avoid wearing expensive jewelry.
- Stick to busy tourist areas, especially at night. Areas in which to be especially careful include the Tenderloin (between the Theater District and Civic Center), the Western Addition (west of the Civic Center) and the upper Mission District (east of Valencia Street).
- Stay awake when riding on public transportation, and keep packages close by. Muni and BART vehicles are equipped with devices that enable riders to notify personnel as soon as an emergency arises.
- Always park your car in a well-lit area. Close windows, lock doors and place valuables in the boot. If someone rear-ends your car, don't stop. Head to the nearest police station or commercial area.
- Never open your hotel room door to anyone of whom you are suspicious.
- If you are confronted by a

mugger, hand over whatever is demanded. Keep a small wad of notes handy as a precaution; this might be sufficient to satisfy the mugger.

If your passport is stolen, report it immediately to the police and your nearest consulate. Keep travelers' cheques (cheques) separate from the list of numbers; in case of theft, report the loss promptly.

Disabled Visitors

By the standards of most other countries, the US provides exceptional facilities for the disabled, thanks to the 1990 Americans with Disabilities Act. Much public transport is equipped to take wheelchairs, and attendants traveling with disabled people can often travel free. In San Francisco, all BART trains and stations, and most Muni lines, are wheelchair-accessible.

All public buildings are (by law) wheelchair-accessible and must provide suitable toilet facilities (although historic buildings are exempt). Most street-corner curbs slope for easy access. Public telephones are easy to reach, and there are special stalls in public lavatories, Braille indicators in elevators, and an increasing number of reserved parking places.

Most popular attractions have handicapped facilities and try to provide necessary comforts. Tourist offices (*see Tourist Information*) have relevant information for disabled travelers, and telephone books list support groups catering for the disabled.

Larger hotels have specially designed rooms which should be booked in advance. Major car-rental firms provide cars with hand controls at no extra cost, although these are limited and early booking is advised.

A Wheelchair Rider's Guide to San Francisco Bay and Nearby Shorelines provides a wealth of information about Bay Area sights; get it free from the California State Coastal Conservancy ☎ 510 286 1015). For more advice, consult the *Planning Guide for Travelers with Disabilities* ☎ 904 487 1462.

Driving

Visitors must carry a valid driver's license issued by their state or country of residence, as well as vehicle registration and/or rental contract, and proof of car insurance.

Vehicles are driven on the right-hand side of roads. Distances are posted in miles (1 mile = 1.6km). Gasoline (petrol) is sold by the gallon (1 gallon = 3.8 litres) and is cheaper than in other countries. Most self-service gas stations do not offer car repair, although many sell standard maintenance items.

Speed limits on expressways are 65mph (104kph) in rural areas and 55mph (88kph) in urban districts. Speed limits on city streets are 15mph (24kph) in school zones, 25mph (40kph) in residential areas and 35mph (56kph) on major streets. Drivers must always give way to cable cars and pedestrians. Seat belts must be worn by drivers and passengers at all times, and child safety seats are required for children under 4 years old or weighing less than 40 pounds.

Roads are especially congested during rush hours (weekdays 7.30-9am and 4-6pm), so try to avoid driving during these times.

Public parking lots are expensive. Street parking, which may be hard to find, has strict rules; violating them will lead to a ticket or, worse, a tow-away. Restricted parking is indicated by the color of the curb: red (no waiting or parking), yellow or black (loading zone), white (five-minute limit), green (10- to 30-minute limit), blue (disabled parking). When parking on a hill, you must block your front wheels against the curb (toward the curb when facing downhill, away from the curb when facing uphill) and use the parking brake (hand brake). In many districts, parking is allowed by permit only; check street signs carefully. Parking is prohibited during posted street-cleaning times.

Earthquake Precautions

Although severe earthquakes are infrequent, they are also unpredictable, and earthquake precautions are a fact of life in the San Francisco Bay Area. If an earthquake strikes when you are outside, move to an open area away from trees, buildings or power lines. If you are in a vehicle, decrease speed, pull to the side of the road and stop. Do not park on or under bridges; sit on the floor of the vehicle if possible. If you are in a building, stay inside a doorway or sit under a sturdy table. Stay away from windows and outside walls. Remain in a safe place until the shaking stops, and be prepared for aftershocks. If possible, listen to the radio or TV for information.

Electric Current

Voltage in the US is 120 volts AC. Foreign-made appliances may need AC adapters (available for loan at some hotel desks, or for purchase at electrical-goods stores) and North American flat-blade, two-pronged plugs.

Embassies see Consulates

Emergencies

In any emergency, dial ☎ 911

and the appropriate service – police, fire or ambulance – will be summoned immediately. Give directions as accurately and completely as possible, including hotel name, street name and nearest intersection. Emergency call boxes are installed on interstate highways at a 0.5 mile (0.8km) to 1 mile (1.6km) intervals.

Guidebooks see Maps

Health

The US does not have a national health service. Before departing, visitors from abroad should check whether their medical insurance covers doctors' visits, medication and hospital treatment in the US. If it does not, travel insurance is highly recommended, as private health care in the US is very expensive. Travel agents and tour companies will recommend a suitable policy.

Should you have a serious accident during your stay, you will be cared for first and asked to pay later. Keep all receipts so that you can claim back any sums you might pay.

For non-emergency care, look under 'Clinics' or 'Physicians and Surgeons' in the Yellow Pages of the telephone directory, where walk-in medical and dental clinics are listed. For minor problems, pharmacies (drugstores) offer a huge selection of medicines.

Prescription drugs should be properly identified and accompanied by a copy of the prescription. If you will require further medication while abroad, ask your doctor to make out a prescription for the composition of the medicine, not the brand name.

Hours see Opening Hours

Information see Tourist Information

Language

English is the main language spoken in San Francisco, though you will hear a wide variety of other tongues spoken as well – particularly Cantonese and other Chinese dialects in Chinatown, and Spanish among the immigrant populations in the Mission

Resident of North Beach.

District. Foreign visitors, however, are often confused by American terms whose meaning can be quite different from their British counterparts. A few common examples are given below.

American / British English	
apartment	flat
bathroom	private toilet
broiled	grilled
check (dining)	bill
chips (dining)	crisps
closet	cupboard
collect call	reverse charges
cookies	biscuits
do not pass	no overtaking
downtown	town centre
drugstore	chemist
elevator	lift
flashlight	torch
freeway	motorway
French fries	chips
gasoline	petrol
hood (car)	bonnet
line (line up)	queue
no standing	no parking
pants	trousers
purse	handbag
restroom	public toilet
round-trip	return
sidewalk	pavement
subway	underground
to go (food)	takeaway
trailer	caravan
truck	lorry
trunk (car)	boot
turnout (road)	lay-by
wrench	spanner

Lost Property

Report any lost items as soon as you realize they are missing. In hotels, check with the front desk or hotel security. When reporting something left in a taxi, if possible give the taxi identification number, shown on the dashboard and on the receipt. (This is a good reason to keep receipts.) The telephone directory has numbers of taxi companies.

Anything lost on a bus, streetcar or cable car should be reported to the San Francisco Municipal Railway (Muni), 949 Presidio Ave, Room 238, ☎ 415 673 6864; for items lost on a commuter train, contact Bay Area Rapid Transit (BART), 800 Madison St, Oakland, ☎ 510 464 6000.

The police should be informed immediately of any lost travel documents. File a police report if you intend to claim an insurance loss for valuable items. Lost or stolen travelers' checks (cheques) and credit cards should be reported immediately to the issuing company with a list of numbers (*see* **Money**).

Maps and Guidebooks

The *Michelin Green Guide San Francisco* provides detailed maps of various neighborhoods of the San Francisco Bay Area, plus full information on main attractions, museums and other sights.

Free maps and brochures, as well as bus and subway maps, are provided by the main tourist-information centers (*see* **Tourist Information**). Car-rental agencies also provide free maps to help with general route planning and driving.

A large-scale motoring map, which may be purchased from any bookstore, is ideal for serious touring outside the urban area. State and national parks, including the Golden Gate National Recreation Area, issue excellent maps of scenic drives and hiking trails with access.

Medical Care *see* Health

Money

US currency is based upon the decimal system, with 100 cents to the dollar. Dollar bills are all the same size and color – a drab green – so it's important to carefully check the different denominations. They are printed in $1, $5, $10, $20, $50 and $100 bills. Coins are a penny (1 cent), nickel (5 cents), dime (10 cents), quarter (25 cents) and half-dollar (50 cents). There are plans to mint a $1 coin, an experiment that failed once previously.

Most banks are members of the network of Automatic Teller Machines (ATMs) that allow world travelers to withdraw cash using bank cards and major credit cards 24hrs a day. ATMs can also be found in airports, grocery stores and shopping malls. Networks serviced by the ATM are indicated on the machine. To inquire about ATM locations and transaction fees, contact your local bank, the Cirrus network (☎ **800 424 7787**) or the Plus network (☎ **800 843 7587**).

The safest way to carry large sums of money is in US dollar travelers' checks (cheques), which are widely accepted and exchanged, or by using credit cards. Banks, most stores, restaurants and hotels accept travelers' checks (cheques) with picture identification.

In San Francisco, American Express Company Travel Service offices are located at 560 California St and 455 Market St (☎ **415 536 2600**). To report a lost or stolen credit card call:
American Express ☎ **800 528 4800**
Diners Club ☎ **800 234 6377**
MasterCard ☎ **800 627 8372**
Visa ☎ **800 336 8472**

Newspapers and Magazines

San Francisco's two main daily newspapers are *The San Francisco Chronicle* (morning) and *The San Francisco Examiner* (afternoon). The Sunday edition, the *Examiner-Chronicle*, is published jointly and has an extensive arts-and-entertainment supplement.

The leading daily newspaper in the East Bay is the *Oakland Tribune*.

Two weekly alternative papers, *The San Francisco Bay Guardian* and *SF Weekly*, both published on Wednesday, offer different perspectives of the city as well as diverse and comprehensive entertainment sections. These free publications are available in newspaper boxes and cafés.

The Bay Area Reporter and *The San Francisco Bay Times* cater to the gay community. In addition, many neighborhood groups publish papers featuring coming events in their areas.

Two free weekly magazines, *Key This Week* and *Where San Francisco*, offer information on events, attractions, shopping and dining. Both are available at hotels and visitor information kiosks.

Opening Hours

Most **shops** are open Mon-Sat, 9am-6pm; some, especially in tourist areas such as Fisherman's Wharf and Chinatown, open Sundays as well. **Department stores and shopping centers** operate Mon-Sat, 9.30am-8pm, and 11am-6pm on Sundays; many extend their hours between Thanksgiving and Christmas. Major **supermarkets** are open at least Mon-Sat, 8am-10pm (or longer) and 8am-7pm on Sundays; a number remain open 24hrs.

Most **tourist attractions**, including museums, open 10am-5pm. Often they will close one day a week, typically on Monday.

Formal business hours are Mon-Fri, 8am-5:30pm. *See also* **Banks** and **Post Offices**

Photography

Good-quality film and camera equipment are available throughout the San Francisco Bay Area. There are plenty of facilities for fast processing. Save money by buying film from drugstores, supermarkets or discount stores where possible, but check the sell-by dates.

Police

California police are generally helpful and obliging when things go wrong for travelers. In an emergency, you can get a quick response by dialing ☎ **911**.

There are three types of lawenforcement officials in the Bay Area: city police; county sheriffs, whose domains are beyond city limits; and California Highway Patrol, which deals with traffic accidents and driving offences outside city limits.

Postal Services

Post offices throughout the San Francisco Bay Area operate Mon-Fri, 9am-5pm; some are open late on weekdays, and 9am-1pm on Saturdays, with limited services. Stamps may also be bought from machines in post-office lobbies, or from hotels, drugstores or supermarkets.

The main post office is at Seventh and Mission Sts. *Poste Restante* mail should be sent here, addressed: name, Poste Restante (General Delivery), San Francisco, CA 94101. The nearest postal depot to Union Square is inside Macy's department store at 170 O'Farrell St. Mail boxes, painted blue, are on many street corners throughout the Bay Area.

First-class mail rates within the US are 32c for a letter up to 1oz (28g), 20c for a postcard. Overseas mail costs 60c for a half-ounce (14g) letter, 50c for a postcard.

Letters and small packages may be mailed from most hotels. Stamps and packing material may be purchased at convenience and drugstores, and at post offices. Businesses offering postal and express shipping services are located throughout the city (*see Yellow Pages of the telephone directory under 'Mailing Services'*).

For further assistance, call the Postal Service Information Line (Mon-Fri, 8am-6pm): ☎ **800 725 2161**.

Public Holidays

Most banks and government offices in the San Francisco area are closed on the following legal holidays. Retail stores and restaurants often remain open all days except New Year's, Thanksgiving and Christmas. Good Friday (preceding Easter in late March or April) may also be a full or half-day holiday.

New Year's Day 1 Jan
M. L. King's Birthday 3rd Monday in January
Presidents' Day 3rd Monday in February
Memorial Day 30 May (or last Monday in May)
Independence Day 4 July
Labor Day 1st Monday in September
Columbus Day 12 Oct (or 2nd Monday in October)
Veterans Day 10 or 11 November
Thanksgiving 4th Thursday in November
Christmas 25 Dececember

Religion

As a cosmopolitan Pacific Rim city, San Francisco is an international melting pot, with virtually every major religious group represented. Catholic churches, and the many Protestant and Orthodox denominations, are easy to find. So, too, are Jewish, Buddhist, Hindu, Muslim and New Age metaphysical. If you're so inclined, there's even a phone service called Dial A Guru. (See *Yellow Pages of the telephone directory under 'Churches'*).

Sightseeing see Tours

Smoking

Smoking is not widely tolerated in the health-conscious San Francisco area. A California state law passed in 1997 has banned smoking from all public areas, including offices, public transport, restaurants and even bars. Many hotels also are non-smoking. The law's constitutionality is being challenged, but it is indicative of the contempt with which smoking is often regarded.

Stamps *see* Postal Services

Taxes

The California state sales tax is 8.5% (non-reimbursable to foreign visitors); cold food items are exempt. A San Francisco hotel occupancy tax of 14% is not included in quoted hotel rates. Tax percentages in other areas, including East Bay, Marin County and the Wine Country, may vary.

Telephones

The cost for a local call from a pay phone is 25c (nickels, dimes and quarters are accepted). Some public telephones accept domestic or overseas credit cards, and will accept long-distance calling cards. Instructions for their use are listed on or near the phone.

Although most hotels add surcharges for telephone calls, the easiest way to make an overseas call is from an hotel room. Although this is more expensive than using a public telephone, it can save a lot of time and energy. You also can call collect or use your credit card by dialing ☎ 0 for an operator.

To dial abroad direct from a public phone, ☎ 011 plus the country code (UK **44**, Eire **353**, Australia **61**, New Zealand **64**) plus the area or city code and the telephone number. Make sure you have a good supply of money in small coins. The lowest rates for international calls to Europe are in effect between 6pm and 7am, and the same is true for local and long-distance calls within the US.

There are more than 160 area codes in the US. The area code for San Francisco is **415**; for East Bay **510**; for the Peninsula south of San Francisco **650**; for the Wine Country **707**. To call outside your area code, ☎ 1 plus the area code plus number.

For directory assistance, dial the area code you want, plus ☎ **555 1212**. For international directory enquiries ☎ **00**. Unless otherwise indicated, telephone numbers listed in this guide that start with '800' or '888' are toll-free (freephone) in the US only.

Time Zone

San Francisco is on Pacific Standard Time (PST), three hours (-3hr) behind Eastern

Standard Time (EST), and eight hours (-8hr) behind Greenwich Mean Time (GMT). Daylight Savings Time, with clocks advanced one hour, is in effect for most of the US from the first Sunday in April until the last Sunday in October.

Tipping

Tipping is standard practice in the US. Hourly wages in the service-industry are relatively low, and many workers count on tips to raise their income to a comfortable level.

In restaurants, it is customary to tip food servers 15-20% of the bill, bartenders and cocktail servers 10-15%. At hotels, tip porters $1 per suitcase, maids $2 per day of occupancy, doormen $1 for hailing a taxi. Taxi drivers are usually tipped 15% of the fare, rounded up to the nearest dollar. Hairdressers and barbers are tipped 10-20%.

Toilets

Public toilets are rare in San Francisco. Except for a handful of stalls on Market Street, and sometimes poorly-kept restrooms in parks, there are none. Department stores and shopping malls, large hotels and fast-food restaurants are good alternatives. Although small shops, restaurants and bars invariably have toilet facilities, use by non-customers is discouraged.

Tourist Information

The San Francisco Convention & Visitors Bureau (201 Third St, Suite 900, San Francisco, CA 94103 ☎ **415 974 6900**), is the main source of tourist information. Its primary Information Center is located on the lower level of Hallidie Plaza at Market & Powell Sts, not far from Union Square. The office is open year-round (Mon-Fri, 9am-5.30pm, Sat 9am-3pm, Sun 10am-2pm ☎ **415 391 2000**). The helpful, multilingual staff are well equipped to assist visitors. In addition, the center stocks brochures for area restaurants, hotels, clubs and attractions, and sells Muni maps and passes.

The Peace Pagoda, Japantown.

Other visitors bureaux in the Bay Area include:

Berkeley Convention & Visitors Bureau 2015 Center St, Berkeley, CA 94704
☎ **510 549 7040**

Visitor Marketing, City of Oakland 250 Frank Ogawa Plaza, Suite 3330, Oakland, CA 94612
☎ **510 238 2935**

Marin County Convention & Visitors Bureau 1013 Larkspur Landing Circle, Larkspur, CA 94939
☎ **415 499 5000**

Napa Valley Conference & Visitors Bureau 1310 Town Center Mall, Napa, CA 94559
☎ **707 226 7459**

Sonoma County Tourism Information 401 College Ave, Suite D, Santa Rosa, CA 95401 ☎ **707 524 7589**

San Mateo County Convention & Visitors Bureau 111 Anza Blvd, Suite 410, Burlingame, CA 94010
☎ **650 348 7600**

You can get statewide information from the **California State Division of Tourism**, 801 K St, Suite 1600, Sacramento, CA 95814 ☎ **800 862 2543**.

Tours

Numerous companies offer **bus tours** of San Francisco's main attractions, sometimes tacking on excursions out of the city. For something memorable, consider a **boat cruise** from Fisherman's Wharf, including panoramic views of the city skyline, Golden Gate Bridge and Alcatraz. Tours are available in several languages besides English.

Specialty tours cater to interests in neighborhoods (such as Chinatown), the arts (literature, architecture, outdoor murals), history and food. Many of these are selective walking tours. Details can be obtained from the Visitors Bureau (*see* **Tourist Information**) or from tourist publications such as *Key This Week* and *Where San Francisco* (*see* **Newspapers and Magazines**).

Transport
see **Enjoying Your Visit, p.95**

TV and Radio

Eleven television stations and more than three dozen AM and FM radio stations are located in the San Francisco area. All major nationwide TV networks are represented, while cable television offers a burgeoning variety of choices.

Radio stations tend to specialize in a particular genre of music, or offer talk shows or continual news. The most varied programming is perhaps provided by National Public Radio; it is carried in the Bay Area by KQED, 88.5FM, and KALW, 91.7FM, both of which also feature BBC broadcasts from the UK.

INDEX

INDEX